MENTAL Utopia

Michael Clemons

Order this book online at www.trafford.com
or email orders@trafford.com

Most Trafford titles are also available at major online book retailers.

Printed in the United States of America.

ISBN: 978-1-4669-4804-4 (sc)
ISBN: 978-1-4669-4803-7 (e)

Trafford rev. 07/18/2012

www.trafford.com

North America & international
toll-free: 1 888 232 4444 (USA & Canada)
phone: 250 383 6864 ♦ fax: 812 355 4082

Contents

Introduction

When those who are called authority figures give mandates that fail to represent any values non-conformists to such mandates find acceptable to comply to, and anger/anguish arises in an authority figures mind from any deviation from compliance to their mandates, I believe that anger exudes of the quality of absurd foolishness, and caters to what people call irrational. Do you find it hard to believe a person might react to social mandates in a questioning manner instead of mere obedience and still be able to enjoy the freedom to think and act in different styles of human intercourse from what is said to be orthodox for the society he or she lives, while fully able to achieve their goals for the fulfillment of job obligations or personal benefit? Moreover, are you offended by those people who live and work in your towns, other towns, or other nations, that have customs or ways of behavior that you just don't understand how they could practice such deviation from how you were raised? Why?

My manuscript, Mental Utopia, will attempt to bring to attention how behavioral idiosyncrasies of people do not have to cause grief and anger among those who are committed to preserving the style of culture they are used to.

Mental Utopia will address issues that might seem provocative to both non secular and secular types, and will offer suggestions on how to maneuver what's seen as crisis into a state of mental well-being, while attempting to evoke an intellectual evolution not only in our educational system, but many areas of government process as well.

The values of educators, doctors, and some that represent what Western civilized communities may call aristocrats are put to test as Mental Utopia will analyze the roles of those said to be leaders in order to see if those people are accomplishing priorities that are descriptive of how their job titles say they are to function, or are just leaders in name only.

The so called authority figures you swear by may be the persons you have come to trust, but who can guarantee the word of an authority figure is unquestionably the most effectual way for you as an individual to achieve your goals? Is there a reason for you to settle for the same value system for your life all of your life if you aren't truly comfortable with the way you're living? Was your happiness determined by what others said was esteem, or didn't you notice that the wants of the land were at one time the wants of just one person with a blueprint? Who says you can't have your own blueprint, with your name on that blueprint as the author? Who can guarantee you have to die mentally anguished at the hands of others who don't share your interests? Please read further . . .

Chapter 1

An Attempt at Reform of the Educational System in America and Beyond

Competency in job function is highly stressed in American educational institutions. Yet many of the leaders of these American educational institutions continue to sanction as mandatory curriculum ideals that foster obsolete sophisms that I believe blind many students to objective thought processes. The word logic is said of how people might have acquired what is more practical for themselves in pursuit of goals, but since what's practical isn't really proven to be the same for all people, then a more realistic method of thought is needed instead of suppositions of the concept of practical as being mostly of similar value among all people, which may cause some people tension when they are confronted by others whose morals and behaviors are different. U.S. Education Secretary Arne Duncan said the United States needs to establish one set of academic standards rather than 50 different sets of academic standards; one national exam aligned to the same standard of academic achievement in all 50 states. Perhaps the same text materials are needed in all U.S. schools. Academic achievement of students is measured based on students proficiency skills in generalized areas. My concern is that some of what educators say is proper criteria for measuring students academic progress is only measuring obsolete concepts that make for perspectives that are not empiricism based. Empiricism is to experiment (question) before making conclusions about an object, not to determine the nature of an object by supposition or theory, for what is the most rational way of approaching a subject or object for an individual. Doing what successful authority says may be rational, but not empirical. There may be more efficient ways of solving problems. Empiricism may help. Educators can't assume students are empirical when not specializing in empiricism.

I am prepared to give you readers some idea of what areas I believe need to be addressed for a more successful educational curriculum for the United States and the Earth. From this point on I will present my claims in a manner that I believe you will view as empirical rather than sophist to show how empiricism is a more rational outlook for not only students, but for all mankind. Rational thought is an essential for mental utopia, and what's practical for the individual.

For those who say English literature/race literature should be a part of the curriculum of most educational programs, I believe English literature only caters to fantasy, and has no more value in creating in students skills in critical thinking/empiricism styles for problem solving than Porky the Pig comic books. I can see a need for English composition courses for future journalism students, but reading of English literature doesn't guarantee skills in writing literature. Another claim by some educators is that English lit/race literature somehow represents diversity among different subspecies/races and helps 'broaden the horizons' of the student, perhaps enlightening students minds for them to better cope with the world. Prove that all people of the same race/ethnic group will act in the same lifestyles or mannerisms as their own kind for fictional tales based on race to represent anything in a students day-to-day real life dealings. If race literature students read is non-fiction, how do the experiences of the author of such literature guaranteed have anything to do with what students experience throughout the course of students lives? If fiction literature is phased out of elementary/high school and college/university, then more time can be given to math. Schools need to promote critical thinking in students so as to help create a more objectivist environment for problem solving. I also believe that critical thinking courses should be mandatory in high schools worldwide. I took a look at a movie called 'American History X'(1997). I believe that the movie had a scene where a father told his children not to take Black literature as seriously as the 'right literature'. The movie fails, in my opinion, to point out that literature classes about any race usually don't prepare students for careers in medicine or engineering and don't offer many job skills, and lit class doesn't prepare students for proficiency in critical thinking. For students seeking to attend university in California, as of year 2000, without critical thinking class credits students are not allowed entrance into the California State university system no matter how good their grade point average is.

My response to some people seeing the need for any countries educational system continuing to value courses in non science history is that knowing a nation's religion and culture will not guaranteed stop egoism of men to ensure any effectuality in stopping wars on this Earth. Also, history classes that are non science are no more than inertia, and aren't designed to instill in students the powers of objective thought for non bias study of social mores.

I feel that a lot of concepts I heard while going to school were based on no more than suppositions. My society has preconditioned some to believe they need to feel things like anger. Even if man can control a certain amount of physical/chemical reactions, probable is still a presumptuous idea. Prove without theoretic that many human emotions said to exist are a naturally occurring part of any human life, as if all peoples values are the same. Can you prove the emotion of anger is natural when it hasn't been proven that all humans experience the same emotions or degree of emotional response to objects external to the human brain as the next human is said to be able to experience? How do you guaranteed feel what someone said you will feel just because you're human? Can you prove that I will feel humbled by my failures when supposed to isn't proven to be tangible existence for me to feel sorry for myself or others? Supposed to is usually no more than words that you might either choose to obey or decide not to obey at all. Think that you are special in the universe. If you see yourself as the most important thing to care for in life, then you don't really see anything as great as yourself, so why would you have regrets when things don't go your way, as if you need some object inferior to yourself for pride and happiness? If you have no regrets, how will you have hatred, or be a victim? Empirical reasoning is to question conventions.

I don't recall any high school or university courses prompting students to think in any way that focuses on improving self esteem. I have seen outlines of Ayn Rand books at bookstores located near the University of Cincinnati campus that do supply books for class instruction at that school. Ayn Rand books are mainly concerned with fostering egoism in people.

When you embraced grief or anger, I believe it wasn't a rational act, and you were only imitating someone else who had grief or anger in response to loss of pride in their life instead of facing reality knowing life has no guarantees. Why are you going to resort to loss of pride just because things went different than you had planned? Surely your pride is more than that of a victim, right? You were not given irrefutable proof that you were supposed to be hurt by anything, not from any chemistry or psychology text. So, why do you let people make a fool out of you and let people control your happiness, when you and your happiness are more important than anything or anyone?

Literature in schools, and also television programs, are proliferate in ideas of tragedy. I believe another way to eradicate grief out of posterities minds is for schools to eliminate the concept of death and loss as tragedy and view luxury as no more than an illusion. How can luxury be only an illusion? Let me explain . . . If men with nothing but a welfare check are glad of that life and glad to get that much, then choose not to pursue free college grants or try for employment and are satisfied, or, I drink a $300.00 bottle of wine and then say the wine was garbage because I don't like wine or need it, then prove there is agreement on what's luxury. One man's god is another man's dog: what is luxury to some isn't luxury to all. In that case, how is there luxury period, instead of what is practical for you as an individual? Why suffer over gain or loss? Luxury and squalor are just mere words when I like what I get and afford, and if that's the case, then someone who says that theirs is better than mine is not guaranteed to prove such. Is life better for you when what I get is practical and I am satisfied with it? Who needs more than what is enough for the individual to have to fulfill human physiological needs to be able to feel happiness? People may think that more than enough is luxury, but in reality it's being practical, and being practical again is not the same for all people. Be rational for the practical.

All the things man says are tragedies are not guaranteed mental pain for any and all humans, so why let suppositions of tragedy make a fool of you? Ideas of tragedy are perpetuated by wallowing in anti-scientific forms of history compared to evolution in raising self-esteem and the level of science technology. You usually have physical comfort no matter what amount of money you have. Money doesn't guaranteed buy you respect, though some people I've met act like it. So much for tragedy. And respect might not be needed, but it might earn trust. To question life's so called trials is empirical. Doesn't that seem practical?

I've lived in many different cities in America, and everywhere the local newspapers are constantly full of reports of drug abuse. Many times I put drugs before rent and food and I've seen it happen to many other people. I was just another weak-minded alcohol and drug addict for many years, going thru life abusing drugs until I had no house purchases, car, or wife. Even though I had university education, I continued to live my life abusing drugs. But one day I looked at my predicament more closely, and thought for a minute. Then I came up with the idea that no conventionalism should be engaged in without questioning it, no matter what that convention or habit was. At that point I said no to the habit that had me thinking I needed drugs to the extent where I lived tired all the time from drug abuse. I said no to settling for going to the park bench or going hungry just to fulfill drug habits that had gotten completely out of control. I said no to continuing to associate myself with people that didn't care for me for friendship or sex unless I conformed to them and used drugs. I said no to the convention that racism needed to continue to be the criteria for my decisions as to whom to associate with. I said no and put an end to my supposition that those who claim to know what is best for me couldn't be flawed in their judgments, just because they have some type of letters or degrees. That line of thought helped put me on the path to empiricism.

You might wonder how not to be brainwashed into the complacency of engaging in activities that you feel are not in your best interest when you are only human. A lot of people believe that you will be subject to the same likes and wants that many people may have because of emotion. You weren't born knowing what hatred is, or born offended by sex with different races/ religions/nations. So how can you not know how to be rational, like before you were told that you needed to be hateful of anything? How can you practice racism without trying interracial sex with all races for yourself, instead of believe in race bigots who don't prove race mixing is detrimental to medical science? When I was a university student in the chemistry department, the way to think was hands on experience, or "I'll be the judge of it" (an example of using empiricism; empiricism is very practical). No one else can know what's right for you if you already know for yourself, from your own experiments(empiricism). What other emotion would you have to experience if you can start to view the world with objective realism, and can also see that most emotions that irritate seem brainwashed into people by a manipulator who wants things to go their way for their selfish ends, except happiness from physical comfort? Do you see any reason for grief? Where is the proof that mental anguish/ anger will exist outside of other peoples minds? Or, that pain really ever needed to exist in your mind? As of 2006, colleges and universities I went to weren't known by me to stress what I preach. Today's student, police officer, and military might benefit from an empirical outlook on life and learn to conquer lack of self-esteem and fear. I don't believe many high schools and colleges are providing the style of mental discipline that I offer here, from which I benefit much happiness.

Do you have to hate what's not practical for you to patronize? Do you have to hate at all? Prove that the police or the judge hates you when they convict you of transgression against the state. I want people as egalitarians not living in animosity. As an egalitarian you should want to see people succeed in maintenance of Western civilization, with empiricism and science technology for convenience. I want egalitarians to take it upon themselves to be more concerned with the welfare of all societies. All schools need to teach this.

A lot of people I know who are university educated walk around claiming that anyone of their own race is intellectually and physically superior to any of the other races, like race guarantees prowess in chemistry/medicine. We need much more objective thought process than 3 year olds these days. Why would you be offended by interracial sex, or homosexuals, if you are supposedly intellectually superior to those types? Hurt is not pride. And then whoever programmed you to be racist or homophobic or hatemonger against some group different than you may not have proven that group was out to destroy you. If a different race or sexual persuasion were truly out to destroy me, you or I really couldn't know or prove whether my enemy was the enemy because of race or sexism, or whether racism/sexism was just a front to intimidate me into obedience. Our enemies might be angry with us, or faking anger to get our obedience. Without self-esteem, you might be miserable at life even without having enemies. With self-esteem, you should be happy even if you do have enemies. To question is empirical. Empiricism should be in all schools.

Today's United States educational systems sociology texts claim to know how different subspecies/subcultures will act according to the particular circumstances. Who can predict if an individual will act the same as one of his/her own subspecies/subcultures at any given time or at all, when two people of the same subspecies/subcultures are subjected to the same social circumstances? In some sociology texts, the author claims there's no such thing as pure blood human races, but I have had a girlfriend with a green birthmark on her foot who said her birthmark was the mark of a pure blood Irish people. And how do you explain one blue eye/one brown eye in the same White race head, like a girl I used to work with, and David Bowie (the rock star). I believe those type of birthmarks are only found on true White races. Some college deans sanction blind sophisms in some text materials and try to pass that off as sound minded critical thinking. Sociology texts are based on presumption, and why should society live their lives according to stereotypes that we don't need to live?

You might say what I'm telling you is the act of a 'liberal'. But, if you are truly one of rational thought, then you will understand when I say that people don't do what's conservative or liberal, they choose to do, or want to do, what they consider practical for themselves. You can't measure conservative/ liberal with gram weight/molecular weight calibration instruments that measure solids/liquids/gases. You can measure practical. And, one man's god is another man's dog: what is right for you may be wrong for me, and vice versa. What I have just explained to you in this section of Mental Utopia I really believe is very important for students as they seek to succeed in the world. I really hope that whoever reads my statements here will get something out of what I have written. I have encountered those who were rigid minded in the opinion that reform of society was no more than a 'pipe dream'. Western civilization was no more than an ideal at one time. But, you're not going to let the cynicism of 'pipe dream' remarks relegate you into inertia, are you? Nothing ventured, nothing gained. Empirical objectivism for rationally practical.

Don't settle for just being a leader in name only. Seek evolution in technology of Western civilization, and rational thought from all people. Please examine the statements that follow . . .

Chapter 2

EXAMINING SOME PROCESSES IN BEHAVIORAL STUDIES

I view the use of psychology and psychiatry classes by the United States educational system and the educational systems of other nations as an attempt to make these schools of thought a helpmate to medical professionals. Psychology and psychiatry are sometimes seen by me as sort of many cultures ideal of the good Samaritan, as well as a preventive measure to try to curtail deterioration of harmonious behaviors among humanity.

Many psychology and psychiatric texts have defined behaviors not adherent to social mores and taboos of a culture as part of some type of brain tissue dysfunction. If your social conduct is different from the society you live, does that prove you're brain damaged? Most mental patients I've talked to had no actual CAT scan or magnetic resonance imaging done on them and are still called under the influence of some type of brain tissue dysfunction. When psychiatrists do blood tests and say mental illness is due to chemical imbalances in humans (missing brain chemicals), the medications given to alleviate brain chemical imbalances usually have no chemicals found naturally occurring in human brain tissue. Therefore, how do you repair so called dysfunctional brains with chemicals that do no more than sometimes sedate you and don't contain brain essentials for the restorative? A number of anti-psychotic medications used by doctors have been said to be quasi effectual to give mental patients who suffer relief, but some anti-psychotic medications have deadly side effects. Doctors may have found differences in the brain/blood chemical makeup of mental patients compared to non mental patients, but are these differences influential when the psychiatrist has no proof that differences in brain/blood chemicals make for hallucinations, or that mental patients even suffer or experience hallucinations at all?

Blood tests done on mental patients I know which were ordered by their family doctors had not disclosed brain/blood chemical deficiencies to these mental patients; I would think a mental patient's family doctor would want to inform their patients of these supposed deficiencies, as such deficiencies are said by doctors to effect critical thinking/decision making faculties. I would want to know . . . if you're a mental patient, wouldn't you want to know?

Psychology/psychiatry texts appear to be in many cases the antithesis of what empirical scientists would call credible scientific research, and not even worth the time of the American Medical Association.

Read further as I explain and identify the many sophisms involved in research of the mentally ill, and offer my idea of what I consider a more empirical approach to studies and assessment of mental patients in the pursuit of peace of mind for the mental patient . . . for mental utopia . . .

Once again on blood testing of the mentally ill . . . I've talked to people who had blood tests for prostate cancer when visiting their family doctor, then were told to check with their urologist for a second opinion when initial prostate blood tests were a little adverse. Now, if a second opinion is sometimes necessary with prostate blood tests, then why not, after a psychiatric blood test, have another blood test given for blood/brain chemical imbalances to mental patients that is sanctioned by their family doctor? Is the word of a family doctor less credible than the word of a psychiatrist? Both psychiatrist and the family doctor use chemist lab test results.

Newsweek magazine reports in the October 12, 2009 issue that psychologist Timothy B. Baker of the University of Wisconsin says that many clinical psychologists "give more weight to personal experiences than to science", and "patients have no assurance that their treatment will be informed by science." Walter Mischel of Columbia University says there is a "widening gulf between clinical psychology practice and science." Thanks to clinical trials some doctors now believe cognitive-behavior therapy (teaching patients to think about their thoughts in different ways and to act on these different ways of thinking) is effectual against depression, panic disorder, bulimia, obsessive- compulsive disorder, and posttraumatic-stress disorder. Multiple trials show that cognitive-behavior therapy brings more benefits with lower relapse rates than drug therapy. The last sentence diminishes the credibility of chemical imbalances as a culprit in mental illness, except in cases of Alzheimer patients or dementia with or without Korsokoff's syndrome.

Yet while doctors have claimed to be treating 'disorders', I fail to see how so called deviant behaviors fall under the category of brain damage. Let us examine the term neurosis. Neurosis is said to be mental illness marked by anxiety and obsessive-compulsive acts supposedly from a disorder of the brain, but usually without organic changes in brain tissues. Therefore, if no brain tissue damage in most neurosis, psychiatrists are not guaranteed sure as to where their patients idiosyncrasies are coming from. Bi-polar syndrome is said to be a neurosis that comes from a genetic defect, but doctors don't know exactly what specific genetic defect that is. Symptoms of Bi-polar syndrome such as inflated self-esteem, excessive talkativeness, racing thoughts, activities done to excess, do not seem to me to be anything I would call mentally ill. Who doesn't want to defeat inertia and stay on top of things? What is mental illness about inflated self-esteem? Depression and suicidal thoughts are also said to be a part of supposedly excessive mood swings of Bi-polar patients. Resonance imaging tests are said to detect abnormalities in the white matter of the brain in Bi-polar patients. Yet scientists haven't explained how people who used to be diagnosed as Bi-polar and now aren't (myself included) can be cured if scars stay on their brain for life if scar tissue is really the culprit in Bi-polar disorder. Can you experience manic-depression or neurosis if those play acts were never described to you? Why be a victim of things you cannot prove you have to feel?

August 2002 Time magazine says some psychiatrists say Bi-polarism is caused by a lack of serotonin, a brain neurotransmitter chemical. February 5, 2005 New Scientist magazine reports that no amount of serotonin depletion has been proven to cause depression. NBC Nightly News came out with a report in 2010 that says the amount of serotonin in human brains cannot be measured by lab technicians. Therefore, how can a lack of serotonin even be measured for psychiatrists to suggest that they have reason to believe serotonin deficiencies cause Bi-polarism, or that what doctors call brain dysfunction has anything to do with chemical imbalances or even exists at all? Are we being lied to by psychiatrists? Again, television news reports say serotonin levels in human brains cannot be measured, so at what point does serotonin become deplete in humans? Neurosis seems nothing more than how people were educated and manipulated, and has nothing to do with any tissue damages or shortages at all.

The Greek philosopher Epictetus said "it's not the thing in itself that troubles us, but our opinion of things. It's not what happens to us, but how we interpret it". If your eye lacks reception to pick up certain wave lengths of light you will live in a colorless world. And depending on the diversity of your I.Q., you will only interpret the external to the extent of your I.Q. That makes your behavior what it is.

Schizophrenia is said to be incongruence to logic, with delusions and hallucinations present. Logic is said to be to do what's practical. But all people don't agree as to what's practical. All people don't take the same approach to money making. If people don't find practical to be the same value among every person, then logic doesn't exist as being the same in all peoples mind. At that point, empirical thought may exist, but not logic. If you can't tell what's logic, then no schizophrenia. To question is practical(empirical).

How do you explain hallucinations? Can you prove voices and visions are not from God or Satan? We can't prove hearing voices/seeing visions exists.

According to February 5, 2005 New Scientist magazine, a doctor has said that schizophrenics have more RNA molecules in their blood/body system than non schizophrenics do. Can this doctor prove that all people with supposedly more RNA in their blood will guaranteed turn out to become schizophrenics, or complain of having the so called symptoms of schizophrenia?

A college teacher of mine told my class that people with large amounts of serotonin are introverts. Well, researchers say no lab test can measure serotonin levels. Are deans at U.S. learning institutes aware of this?

The behavior of people that is not civil minded behavior style looks to be no more than egos bigger than those who are offended by behavior said to be uncivilized. Are you going to let psychiatric sophisms of 'delusions of grandeur' rob you of your self-esteem? Just what are you supposed to be scared of when a so called scientist labels you paranoid schizophrenic because you told him you were hearing voices? Were you scared by something so badly that it made you hear voices? Sounds like an irrational claim of absurdity. This might seem absurd also . . . I have been told by some people that they didn't start hearing voices (a sacrilege) until they tried anal sodomy. Now, according to the Physicians Desk Reference, 22.4 milligrams of Stelazine, Navane, Zyprexa, Thorazine, or 3 to 5 milligrams of Seroquel will induce necrospermia. Necrospermia is the inability of sperm to fertilize female eggs (dead sperm). Clozaril and Mellaril will keep males from ejaculating period. All of the medications listed directly above are anti-psychotic medications. If sperm is already dead or absent during anal sodomy because of anti-psychotics, then you haven't properly accomplished the death of seed by anal sodomy, which just about completes an act of sacrilege.

Some mental patients say they hear voices of people that they are, or used to be, friends with. The voices are usually said to be telling mental patients to come and have anal sex with the person whose voice the patients say they hear. The voices are said to be saying to have anal sex with one or more of the persons throwing the voices so it can be shown to the person saying they hear voices how to turn these voices on and off. It's up to the mental patient saying that they hear voices to choose whether to have condom-less anal sex or not. Absurd? You be the judge.

Does supposed hearing of voices keep people from problem solving and thinking and establishing valid arguments for their decisions? I've never heard of people who said they hear voices not able to work or not able to establish their goals they set for themselves.

Schizophrenia to me is no more than some people are more zealot than others without regard to what other people think or feel. If schizophrenia is the impractical, then if you flunk math you should be schizophrenic. But of course, that is not the case. It would seem schizophrenia doesn't exist.

Anti-psychotic drugs like Seroquel actually increase hypertension and will cause arrhythmias in some heart patients; arrhythmias in hypertension patients may cause death. Anti-psychotic pills like Zyprexa cause obesity, and diabetic and heart patients cannot afford to be obese, as obesity in diabetic and heart patients can lead to amputations and/or death. Medication like one called Depakote may have side effects where inflammation of the intestines occurs, which can result in death. If any mental patients are reading this, I would suggest that you take Navane or Stelazine for insomnia; they have very few side effects. Dalmane is also good for sleep, has few side effects, and will sedate you properly, since barbiturates are reserved for epileptics these days. I'm told that most of the major complaints of mental patients are concerning inability to sleep at night, not how they are incapable of thinking in a manner productive for themselves.

A psychiatrist might give 10 different anti-psychotic medications to a patient in a 5 year period. In other words, if one pill doesn't work, try another one. If the so called psychosis is said to be a chemical imbalance, then wouldn't the same medication every time be beneficial to every and all psychotic patients said to be afflicted with the same particular disease? Are we supposed to believe that some peoples brains are made out of different chemicals than the rest of humanity? Is so called excessive RNA supposed to be reduced by anti-psychotic medications, and where is the proof that any anti-psychotic medication will reduce excessive RNA or will compensate for excess RNA?

I don't believe people have to suffer when they or others are deemed neurotic or psychotic. You may have been programmed into conforming to things that are said to be acceptable ways of behavior by people that have no proof that you needed to act any way at all towards humanity. You have no proof that you need to love what humanity loves, or live the way humanity lives.

A lot of English dictionaries contain words that describe ideas that are used as control devices by people who have taken it upon themselves to get some person or groups obedience. Words like respectable/vulgar, tame/wild, lazy/arrogant, conservative/liberal, probable, modern(when you can't create matter) . . . do those words describe tangible reality? Do you assume without any empirical questioning that those type of words are practical for you as an individual to conform to them? I will explain how those words, and others as well, actually have no basis in reality, and don't describe anything that truly exists later on in this book. For now, I have something else I feel you will find interesting . . .

Here is some thinking which gives me feelings of well-being; I'd like to present this for the benefit of mental patients and everyone . . .

There is a concept called nihilism where its practitioners believe life has no value or importance. The nihilist may also attempt to destroy what is said by the nihilist to be of inferior quality in form or concept, so as to send a message to society that even if society conforms to said inferiority, the nihilist won't. If there's nothing important about the existence, then how will there really ever be anything important enough for people to experience hate, resentment, and mental anguish? Then thoughts said to be inferior are now regarded as obsolete, and left behind. With the comfort and convenience bourgeoisie have given to Americans, there's no real need for hate and anguish even if things are labeled important. While I enjoy the level of civilization bourgeoisie have made for Americans, that doesn't mean I need to be content with what I get, as if I have proof things cannot be better. Therefore, I can be nihilist and seek to reconstruct my environment into something more pleasurable if such can be had: Just because I like what bourgeoisie does for Western civilized nations doesn't mean I have to give their gift to mankind importance in order to have pride.

Now I can be nihilist and seek to expose as sophism concepts of sacred and evil as God and Satan cannot prove that it is right for me to obey them, and can only dictate their will while I have a choice to obey or not. How do I know men can and do speak for God and Satan? With a nihilist perspective, I can chose empiricism with religion and give importance to nothing but that which serves bourgeoisie on the Earth for more convenience for humanity and what serves Jesus also, or I can give nothing importance, or be a vigilante for some values that I may have or seek that serve my comfort while I'm still on Earth. Now I can concentrate on what's practical versus impractical for myself, instead of concentrating on others out to blind me with concepts of insanity and sanity. I can choose what I think is success for myself on my own. And, no convention without question, while constantly questioning my own value system to see if my choices are conducive of what I feel I can truly say is success for myself, not relying on sympathy for or from others. I feel empathy, but not sympathy.

I believe nihilism can put my life in a perspective where even if I don't get what I do want, I am not hurt when others get what they want. I'm happy, and I don't let sophisms of luxury(one man's idea of rich is another man's idea of poor) stop me from seeing life as a road to nowhere, where I might not look like or seem like anyone important to people at all, but I'm always aware that I'm not missing anything I need or didn't already have: peace of mind over the temporal.

Some people may have more money than you, millions of dollars perhaps, but that doesn't make luxury if you are physiologically contented with what men said is poverty. How are people with more money than you going to prove they are better off in life than you? Is their bed and food proven better than yours? You are not rich or poor . . . you have the amount of money that is practical or impractical for you to have. Everyone's idea of practical isn't proven the same.

Any nihilism you might feel should not be based on cynicism; perhaps a person whom you haven't met before comes along and has some value to you, value that may give your society some importance. Cynicism is no more than only a supposition that all people are no good, and supposition has no guarantees and is only a generalization. Just because most people you have encountered so far may be the enemy of you and your plans obviously doesn't prove you'll never have friends. Even if you never need friends, I feel misanthropy is really irrational. And being upset until you hatemonger isn't what I call being prideful. I believe less stress in your life depends on nurturing self-esteem and looking at yourself with empirical thought to the point your life is rational, and you are feeling that you're not making mistakes no matter what your society says of you.

It looks as though psychologists, and maybe even psychiatrists, are not as devoted to science as we were led to believe. In some U.S. mental health clinics, they allow psychiatric nurses to write drug prescriptions for mental patients. What purpose is there for giving psychiatrists more prestige than psychiatric nurses in matters of administering psychotropic drugs for mental patients? Psychiatrists aren't proven anymore knowledgeable in pharmacology than psychiatric nurses or the Physicians Desk Reference, which any mental patient can buy and should read. Your pharmacist is licensed as more qualified to administer psychotropic drugs than a psychiatrist. It doesn't look like the clinical psychologist has very much use to those versed in critical thinking at a high school or college campus, and may as well be considered obsolete. The continued instruction of psychology in any society's schools looks to be no more than sophist when held up to empirical method of thought, and is beginning to look worthless to those who seek true medical professionalism and true science.

Sociology classes in high school/college/university are taught by people who are still conforming to school curriculums that promote collectivist views of people that assume that all people of same culture and race will respond in similar fashion to the same stimuli. That type of collectivism doesn't instill rational, objective thought in anyone.

You can take what I say and apply it to your everyday life if you think it may be of some use to you, whether you have issues with mental health or not. This is part of my approach to life. Perhaps it can work for you. Please read further as I continue to explain my method for mental utopia . . .

Chapter 3

MENTAL UTOPIA

Notice how I constantly refer to the word empiricism. Empiricism involves experiment before conclusion as to the nature of an object or behavior instead of supposition as to the nature of an object or behavior. When you use empirical approaches of thought I believe you seek to serve yourself. Ego may be pride, but are you rational? I believe empiricism should be done for temperance when being egoist. The concept of altruism can be seen as egoism. When doing a supposedly selfless act, you're actually doing it to satisfy your want to help someone. Once you help someone, you are satisfied, and that sense of satisfaction rewards your ego. And to question is the basis of empiricism.

You might wonder how use of empiricism to deal with external to your brain can coincide with religion and still be of value to your decisions. The author Ayn Rand wrote a book called 'The Virtue Of Selfishness' . . . my dictionary says virtue is moral excellence, which includes the concept of being chaste. Chaste is the selfishness of saving yourself in Christ, but unmarried sexual conduct is also selfish, and I don't believe seen as virtuous by Christian churches. Can anyone prove all selfishness is based on obedience to morals in any religions bibles for statements like selfishness is virtue to look like more than just really flippant and sophist, and basically anti-empirical in context? Some orthodox style Christians and Muslims might find empiricism offensive. However, God didn't put you on Earth to be a victim of people's wills that you don't accept. God gave you the will to think for yourself. Again, can you be empirical and also religious? You don't need church and all its rituals to believe Jesus is the only god to obey and to do what Jesus says. Even if you could find some anti empiricism in the King James bible, you don't need to do what that bible says except to serve only the commandments of Jesus for salvation purposes. Then you still serve yourself (empiricism) and also Jesus. Do kindness when appropriate, love Jesus if you choose to be religious, and also look to empiricism to solve problems you may have. I'm hoping people of all religions can see the value of empiricism in problem solving. There may be empiricists that have no person or god before them, then there may be empiricists who have no one before them except the god of their choice. Out of body experiences tell me there is a spirit world, so I don't call religion supposition.

Empirical might be practical, but is all said to be practical empirical? No, because even if you obey race bigotry and stay with your own kind for your parents $300,000.00 trust fund to be given to you, that doesn't make race mixers degenerate in empiricism and unable to excel in medical science or inferior to homogenous biological function between different subspecies (races). Does science guarantee empiricism? No, since there's so far no cure for all disease. Is empiricism a guaranteed constituent of bourgeoisie? Empirical method of thought from yourself doesn't prove you contribute anything to upkeep of any society, but only that empirical thinking is how you chose to cope with your own personal agendas. I do believe aspiring leaders should embrace empiricism for the maintenance and evolution of Western civilization.

Does a concept you value or perhaps see as a contingency for yourself really describe something tangible in existence, or nothing more than words for you to let that concept relegate your behavior into emotions none can prove you need to feel? I don't believe things said to be abstract are guaranteed intellectual preponderance as some dictionaries that I've read claim.

Take all words that offend you that you can find in the unabridged dictionary and ask yourself why they offend you when you have no proof you need to let no more than a word anger you. Abstracts are not concrete objects, and many words that incite anger or fear are not describing anything more than an abstract(intangible). The concept of practical and impractical is some of what determines what behavior is. Tame/wild, respectable/vulgar, holy/evil, lazy/arrogant, conservative/liberal, probable . . . are sophisms. One mans tame is another mans idea of wild, and one mans crimes are seen by another as legit. If all men don't have the same values, then how can mere adjectives describe what's tangible in existence that can be measured (like how nouns label physical objects) for the words tame/wild, respectable/vulgar, psychotic/sane, lazy/arrogant, holy/evil, perversion, and modern(when humans can't create matter) and conservative/liberal to be anything more than ornamental abstracts that can't measure the degree by which all men see things, for you to let these abstract concepts control your behavior into irrational forms of emotion instead of your behaviors determined by rational empiricism? Obviously, abstract concepts are not always seen as intellectual preponderance. I will now gradually explain more about words that are only describing abstracts. The more empiricism I practice, the more well-being I receive.

I always trained myself not to repress my thoughts, even if they were uncomfortable, so I would lose fear of thinking what men told me were taboo thoughts, and in the process I began instilling in myself pride. With less fear comes pride for me, so I can take on things like being the mayor, or the governor, or even the president of my country, or of the Earth. How about you?

Here's something for you to think about . . . not only is tragedy an obsolete concept (because who wants mental cripples?), but has tragedy even needed to exist at all, except that people told you your 'loss' was to be painful, and you believed it because society programmed you to? You're not a true loser unless you regret your decisions. But why does regret sometimes lead to mental pain? If you don't know why mental pain has to exist, then why let it exist? Just because someone in your youth told you mental (and even physical) pain will exist sometimes . . . now you're going to believe it? Try to break away from ideas that there is something wrong with you if you don't feel shame from not feeling pain over so called tragedy. You can't change death off of this Earth, or loss of possessions (except to attempt to recoup), so why hurt because others said you will or need to? You might be called arrogant for being callous and indifferent to pain of others, but you don't guaranteed owe anybody sympathy, and all people may not give sympathy either. Some emotions seem contrary to empirical thought. I have attempted to present what I write about in this book in an empirical manner. People that want you to feel bad because they do aren't empirical in thought. And why would you feel bad that something didn't go your way? It wouldn't be because somebody told you to feel bad about some so called tragedy, would it? Think for yourself before you buy into the concept of what people call tragedy . . . tragedy wasn't originally your idea to begin with.

It would seem that many emotions have no value in an empirical, rational society, and are no more than obsolete, except for happiness. Why is happiness the only emotion that's legitimate for people to actually feel? You were never a victim when you had no regrets . . . regrets you had from giving things more value than yourself. Usually, what many people feel is comfort from food and rest, so all you know is happiness until you were told to believe in fear and hate. So far, I don't regret any situation I've been in. And all I feel is happy. I suggest you consider a semi nihilist approach to life. Is anything more important than yourself or your comfort? With these ideals you're never really a loser, and are surely a winner of peace of mind no matter what your life situation is.

I hope you will come to the conclusion that emotions outside of happiness are paradox, but don't let happiness blind you to empirical, rational analysis. You may get smug with the sense that all is well for you but don't forget not to naively accept convention without question. There may be room for improvement, but you won't know that by being complacent.

To try to alleviate sorrow you should tell people at an early age that all men may think they are better than you and will do as they please, and are going to be totalitarian no matter what. Does that lessen any paranoia you may have when you are told to expect adversity? It toughened me up somewhat. I don't see myself as cynical when I say that I feel desensitized to peoples displays of hate or violence because I expect people to be as totalitarian as I am. My dictionary says anyone that wants things to go their way is totalitarian, but even in an egoist environment I have seen people benevolent toward others. My enemies are something I expect not to cower to me at all, and what I lose is of importance only to the gullible and nothing to be afraid of. If you are as objectivist as I am, you or I couldn't really guarantee things will go our way for you to put that much importance on what is no more then the temporary in the first place for you to be absurd enough to hurt over anything of this Earth, could you? If you have love and sex, you're not guaranteed always going to have them, are you? Also, all things are made up of chemicals, including you. How does loss of control of no more than chemicals that may or may not be part of your physical makeup, chemicals not proven to be any more evolved than yourself, invoke sorrow in rational thinking minds? How many chemicals are there that are greater than the ones that make your soul? Chemicals that are part of the physical structure of the mechanisms of Western civilization may be designed technologically different than before, but their sub-atomic compositions aren't seen as any more valuable than those that make up your sub-atomic composition by you, are they? Now do you feel sorrow will have a place in your life?

How can you be totalitarian when things of this Earth are temporary? You certainly don't let people deprive you of your physical comfort, do you? I don't even know how anyone can take pleasure away from the empirical minded. Sizing up life with emphasis on empirical deduction in thought, all I get is happiness; I don't know how I could be more happy.

Considering totalitarianism, when you are assertive for yourself some people may call that pompous, or arrogant and belligerent. All I believe people are using words like arrogant for are as a control device to get your obedience. You might want to question those that use words like pompous as to what gave them the idea they had the right to establish themselves as authority over you, and have them prove themselves to empirically know what's best for you as an individual. One man's arrogant is another man's idea of being survivalist. You now have more of an excuse to assert yourself, as many take it upon themselves to, for your attempt at what you call success.

If you have a habit of constantly nay-saying and trying to find fault with peoples values that are different than yours when these 'deviants' who are of different values than you are happy with the way they live, and you have no proof of accomplishment that shows lifestyles different than yours are inferior in degree of comfort to what type of lifestyles you live and say that you appreciate, I suspect that your view on what the 'right' way to live just isn't really all the way based on empirical thought. Some people claiming to have 'winners' accomplishments don't seem to realize most folks usually have accomplishments that they call successful living, even though everyone doesn't guaranteed see the same accomplishment as of the constituents of a 'winners' lifestyle. One man's idea of success is not every man's idea of success. Maybe you kissed ass for what you want and perhaps claim that those who didn't kiss ass to get your lifestyle and level of income are not 'intelligent' as you, and are 'losers' in the society you live. It doesn't seem to occur to browbeaters preaching how they are better off than those that don't overtly kiss ass in quality of comfort in life that if the so called loser valued what the so called winner calls success, I'm sure the so called loser would have kissed ass in the first place if they really thought what the supposed winner thinks is royalty is truly royalty.

I seem to think that ice cream tastes just as good to many welfare recipients as it tastes to those that live in Beverly Hills. Don't you? Wishing people feel like they're failures when they look happy doesn't seem like pride.

For those of you who may feel like you have no reason to live . . . if people are said to only get pride from accomplishment, how can you still feel pride with seemingly no accomplishments in your life? Accomplishing peace of mind by not being victims of other peoples differences in race and religion through empiricism gives me pride, more pride than when I was younger and based my pride on the absurdity of racism and supposed preponderance over others through religious rituals or level of income.

How do you know all men call the same thing respectable or vulgar, for either to exist? If you're offended by anything you're not pride in my opinion. Either something happens or it doesn't, so no such thing as probable. If supposed to do/think something cannot be guaranteed to exist, then how does lazy exist, or the concept of perversion measure something tangible? If matter cannot be created or destroyed, then how can there be modernism except for the concept of time in the here and now? All physical matter, according to the reports of some chemists, is trillions of years old. To question is the basis of empiricism.

Don't be an unthinking puppet or victim of those who use words that fail to explain how things are tangible existence. Why base your livelihood on the irrational? If the irrational comes from your family's mouth, try to instruct them in an empirical manner how they aren't delving in reality.

When people say decadent of behavior different from what they are culturally used to, why is anyone's cultural style supposed to stay the same? And for what reason? Is a persons capacity for empirical method of thought somehow eliminated just because that persons artistic tastes have changed due to empiricism into some other value system? I don't know of anyone who has any proof that rational thought will diminish in a person if that person changed their artistic tastes because of empiricism. To wallow in the redundancy of never trying to except views or styles different than ones you were raised to believe in half of your life isn't seemingly the rational objective idea of no convention without question and is inertia, which seems degenerate compared to seeking evolution in intellectualism through empiricism, degenerate as those that live in resentment and perhaps physical pain because of what they label decadent.

A loser mentality is one that the music industry in America perpetuates when the constant themes used by musicians are ones based on concepts of tragedy, loss, fear, and mental anguish, which do not focus on how to beat regret, and not conducive of inspiring rational thought. People who want Western musical cultures to stay the same are possibly doing a blind disservice by not training children to react to absurdist escapism with empirical assessments, because continuing to foster ideals of tragedy doesn't instill pride.

I notice almost every MSNBC report I watch (particularly 5 p.m. est. on) how the journalists are constantly preaching concepts of conservative and liberal. I'd like to show you how rigid parochialism doesn't always seem the accurate way to present things. Earlier on I wrote that people really aren't conservative or liberal, but try to do what is practical for themselves. You can measure what's practical or impractical of objects with gram weight/molecular weight calibration, but you don't measure conservative/liberal in the lab. One man's conservative is another man's idea of liberal. Also, if a person says no to race mixed marriages and is opposed to abortion . . . well, no to race mixing is the same as abortion, and also genocide (of a human race species) and murder. Total race mixing may end pure blood races (genocide?), so you might want sex with empiricists instead of licking race. It seems adhering to conservative/liberal labels can be no more than sophist, with the irrational being passed off as empirical. Prove liberalism of people who listen to 20 year old Front 242 music instead of 40 plus years old Jimi Hendrix music. I believe you measure the value of music by how you were educated and whether the music entertains you, not by the words conservative or liberal, as I've seen 33 to 43 year old men not into shooting heroin into then 5 year old Front 242 music (which is synthesizer and sound effects music with little or no guitars) and 15 year olds that only liked then 25 year old Jimi music; these 15 year olds were living in the streets and shooting heroin. Would you call 1993 33/43 year old synthesizer heads that don't want guitar music but don't shoot heroin liberals, and the 15 year olds in 1993 that still listened to much older Hendrix music and then shoot heroin while homeless the stereotype of what people have called conservative? Neither those 33/43 year olds or those 15 year olds are fitting in with labels of conservative or liberal; they are only acting in ways that are practical for themselves to get some of what they value. If you're into anti abortion and are pro-race mixing you can't be both liberal and conservative at the same time. Furthermore, down with abortion may be seen as liberal for taking liberties to impose giving birth on the pregnant, and pro-race mixing may be considered conservative for being in league with Torah. It seems like conservative and liberal don't really measure anything that exists.

You can support ideas that are inferior to empiricism manner of thought instead of intellectual evolution over sophism, but I believe that clinging to the anti empirical just because you are partial to someone's race, religion, sex gender(or sex act), or looks, or guitar playing ability, or nation, or wealth doesn't make sophist arguments rational, or sophism look anything similar to values people look for when seeking leaders. Do you have to be a leader? No, but leaders that seek evolution of a human race species over famine and disease, the true leaders over what we may have been told were aristocrats on the Earth, are thought to be sought after by the dean of every college and university, as well as those who want to see their society flourish.

I thank those that seek evolution. Those who are empirical are valuable, in my opinion, in an attempt at being a catalyst for evolution.

If you don't value all of the ideals of Western civilization and live in rural Africa, then some American ideals of what's leadership and empiricism may not be anymore to rural Africa than unnecessary. You might remember that empiricism is to experiment, or I'll be the judge of it type of thinking. Some Africans lifestyles that perhaps don't have access to as much Western technology as Americans may have can't really be proven to be anti empirical if native Africans are satisfied as to how they get what they value. Some places in Africa you can use a donkey to get around instead of a Volvo, and you really couldn't guaranteed prove that it was less practical to use a donkey than a Volvo when you got what you wanted out of the donkey, and didn't need/want/afford to assimilate into all of the Western technological styles of living. Your donkey made it from point A to point B effectually. Prove that you need Western civilization and all of it's constituents to assess life in an empirical manner, and that rural Africans ideals of preserving the happiness of their neighbors and the tenets of their culture are any less founded on empirical minded values than what you may experience in America or Australia or Europe. Your idea of practical may not be my idea of practical, but does it need to be?

Are you really anti empirical enough to let yourself be fooled into irrational feelings of shame and regret by other people?

Prove that a person richer than you can guaranteed instruct you on how to be an effectual leader.

Why does a person say they carry the 'weight of the world' on their shoulders just because they were said to be a leader? Does that so called burden sound like cynicism? Does the leader with so called burden from work guaranteed to be more value to mankind than other leaders? Prove all people aren't able to contribute to the upkeep of the society they live as well as the leaders. We have leaders that are functional in upkeep of society, and that's great, but why slander and shit on those who can't excel to a level of prominence? Maligning those who aren't intellectually endowed to be preponderance isn't my idea of empirical thought or a leadership type of quality. You may say you're burdened, but are you guaranteed to have done anything more than obscurity for work records? All job duties of a society aren't only under the jurisdiction of just those said to be authority figures for authoritarians to sophism and bullshit people like society will collapse if it wasn't for the efforts of the so called burdened of authority figures who use the 'weight of the world' rhetoric. I don't consider cynicisms as anything more than sophisms not worthy of empiricists or leaders.

If people persist in attempting to peeve you off with slander or physical abuse, take it that they are your victim, and the fact that they are steadfast and tenacious in their attack on you seems they hurt a whole lot more than they can take. With an empirical approach to the enemy I find I don't have any mental pain no matter how my enemies may live the irrational.

If someone says that their degree of education is more refined than your educational level, ask them to explain as to what degree their cultural idiosyncrasies are superior to the stance of an egoist or an empiricist. Is it proven those claiming to be more refined than you have better prowess in their educational field than you because they learned their skill in school and your knowledge of their field came from the library, or outside of school? Can any school the refined one went to make guarantees that most any of their graduates are socially acceptable to all people, or lucrative to all in their field? Prove the refined ones culture is more effectual in empiricism than you are just because of you being a different culture, perhaps in race or financial background. Degrees from school don't guarantee more money made than the unschooled, or money at all. Prove school is better for collecting pay for art projects than not attending art college for your knowledge in art. I believe the rock artists Prince, Joe Strummer, David Byrne, and David Bowie never graduated a university or college with an art degree, but they were famous millionaires in art unlike many obscure art degree types I've been acquainted with, who graduate art school with general degrees in art/music conservatory and never make the type of money of $2,500.00 a week or more art circles. Usually an art degree bachelor doesn't make $1,000.00 a week most of their career. I've noticed art degree types having contempt for non art degree types as if art degree types guaranteed have most of the productive skills of any and all working people in a society, or will always prove themselves to possess skills that make for leadership. True leaders can use skills of the collective bourgeoisie and organize their talents for jobs completed. As art degrees do not make artists any less human or less worthy of respect, I've been given the snob treatment by artists/musicians/Bachelor of Art degree types and laughed at how they had assumed I would kiss up to their clique as if they were automatically seen by everyone as having some 'weight' on their shoulders of having to tolerate the not so 'vogue' compared to their tastes, where I believe art is only in the eye of the beholder and not agreed on as to its correct constituents by a collective whole of any society.

Can you prove so called culturally refined people are any happier than you are? All the oyster eating in the world is said not to have any of the nutritional value of oatmeal, whether you or anyone likes it or not.

Refining your life with the proper diet and exercise is said to be very essential for a more pleasant life, and perhaps the life of an octogenarian as well. Please read further . . .

Chapter 4

FOR YOUR DIET AND HEALTH

I have some information which I believe is essential for an attempt at a life of good physical health and mental well-being. I'm sharing this info with you because the following diet, health, and exercise habits are how I live, and how I want my loved ones to live. My reward is inner peace, and mental utopia.

Here is how I eat . . . starting with bread and grains, I usually only take wheat bread, as wheat bread is said to be a good source of fiber, which is for proper colon health. Colon cancer death rates are significantly high, so get a colonoscopy every 3 years starting at age 50 for males and females. Bran flake cereal, oat cereal/oatmeal, shredded wheat/wheat cereal are also said to be good for proper colon health. Over 43 years of age may also want to invest in Metamucil for bowel regularity, a sort of cleansing out of the bowels. Another word about wheat bread . . . wheat bread is said to be good for helping to prevent fat buildup on the kidneys, which may lead to kidney cancer. If you can, eat cereals and grains without sugar. Even though oat and wheat cereal is said to be appropriate eating for proper heart health, it would be sort of contradictory to eat sugar-coated cereals, or add sugar to your cereal if you are worried about cholesterol/fat buildup in your heart muscle and circulatory system. I don't add sugar to my diet and that keeps my blood pressure down. Pasta is said to be better than potatoes and white rice for keeping blood sugar and blood pressure low. If you like cookies, try to make those cookies sugar-free, and minus the chocolate and caramel.

It isn't difficult to give up excess sugar in your meals if you put some will-power into it. Try to be bigger than the world.

Concerning meat, consider reducing the amount of meat you eat, as limiting your protein intake may ward off cancer. For the appropriate amount of protein on a daily basis I may eat 60 grams protein per 24 hours, which is all the protein doctors say humans will need to eat. Eating less meat products in your diet, especially beef, is said to be good for proper colon health. Do keep meat a part of your diet. I was told that there was a greater risk of leukemia for vegetarians than for those that consume meat. I prefer poultry and fish for meat, and though poultry and fish are said to be better than beef and pork for your colon and heart health, you may want to be careful of where your fish comes from. High toxicity levels are said of fish coming out of Asian waters(Tilapia). Also, atrophy of brain tissues may occur if you don't get enough protein or salt. Type O positive or negative blood types are needing to keep meat in their diet to help reduce possibilities of cancer. Condiments for your taste . . . mayonnaise, mustard, ketchup, horse radish, and sauces or dressings are not advised as they may contain oils, vinegars, and salt in levels that are not conducive of proper blood pressure/circulatory system health. Consumption of eggs should be minimal as eggs are high in cholesterol, but they do give good protein if you are watching your colon health and want to reduce meat.

Vegetables are always good, and beans are said to be a good way to get protein. Try to get frozen vegetables if you can, as they have less salt. Sweet peas and carrots are good fiber for the colon. While grits are said to be good iron content, my advice is to get your iron from spinach instead. Try to eat some type of vegetable every day for essential minerals. Eating more fruit dishes is said to be better than drinking fruit juice in order to get more fiber, while not eating citrus fruit reduces dentin wear on teeth from citrus juice acid content. Fruit may have anti oxidizing agents that help retain nutrients from other foods. Corn sugar based fruit juice is inferior on your heart compared to natural unsweetened fruit juice.

Here's more about meat . . . you might want to throw away eating of fast food and processed foods (tacos, pizza, hot dogs) because of triglycerides. Triglycerides are fats that are bad for your heart. Processed food includes lunch meats and peanut butter. Peanut butter contains glycosides (sugar that turns to fat) that may contribute to heart disease. It would be safer for your heart to eat whole nut products as they have fats more healthier than triglycerides and glycosides.

Dairy products are high in protein, but if you are lactose intolerant, try soy milk. If you are able to digest milk, stick with 1% low fat milk which is not too much fat on your heart but enough fat for your needs, as your body needs some types of fat. I try to limit the amount of cheese I eat to nothing more than 2 days a week as while cheese is said to be very good for you, cheese is also processed food, which may have glycosides, or even triglycerides. Usually ice cream is good for protein and potassium, but ice cream is also full of glycosides. For proper muscle function(also to eliminate cramps) you want potassium, so try bananas instead of ice cream, salt laden Gatorade, or white potatoes, which are too much sugar for proper blood pressure/heart function. I don't use dairy butter or margarine, which is extra fat we can live without.

Salt is said to be dangerous in excessive amounts, which is over 2000 mg. per 24 hour period, and said to cause much heart disease. I go for salt free foods as much as possible, as I have high blood pressure myself. Caffeine free diets are advised for high blood pressure patients also. There is now caffeine free soda that is sugar free and salt free as well. Saccharin in diet sodas was the only sweetener found cancerous in lab mice. If you don't trust diet sodas enough to continue doing them, you may want to switch to eating fruit or drinking water. You might want to take to more water considering that it is hydration for you with little salt and sugar in it, and usually no caffeine or food coloring. Caffeine may be good for those with no hypertension, but caramel colored sodas were said to be cancerous. The kind of diet I've been describing here works so well for me that I don't even have to take medication for my high blood pressure as long as I closely monitor what I eat and drink.

With or without high blood pressure you should exercise also. We need to exercise at least 2 to 3 days a week for all ages and walks of life. Stretching for about 15 minutes a day is good for circulation: Trunk twisters, toe touches, toe ups, stretching of the external oblique (waist area), jumping jacks . . . follow that with a 45 minute workout on weight machines. Try doing most of your exercise in the mornings. If you don't have access to weight equipment, then after stretching try 37 push ups under 2 minutes and 52 sit ups under 2 minutes, 2 to 3 days a week. Jogging is a good way to lose weight and increase stamina, but jogging is said to be bad for the knees. You might want to try swimming and/or bicycling instead of a jog for muscle tone, increased stamina, and good cardiovascular health in combination with your exercises.

I've been told by my doctor to drink at least 8 16 ounce glasses of water a day, which is said to be a good way to hydrate, and proper flushing of the kidneys. Cranberry juice is recommended for good kidney health and is advised as something to take serious instead of so much soda drinking. Watch out for cranberry juice with corn sweeteners, or flush kidneys with water.

I also suggest that if you want something good for your circulation, try garlic instead of wine. Take clove garlic instead of garlic salt for hypertension.

For men, you may want to have a PSA screening blood test for prostate cancer done every 12 months. Ask your personal physician and a urologist for the test. Don't settle for only a digital rectal exam as it is not conducive of catching improper enzyme formation in prostate tissue, which may prove cancerous. The prostate is to be checked once a year after a mans 40th birthday.

For women, you want your HPV shot and PAP smear every year, no matter what your age in an effort to control cervical cancer. Women need breast exams for cancer every year.

I'm glad I was told there was a vaccine for pneumonia. I didn't hear of pneumonia vaccines until I was over 47 years old. Pneumonia vaccines can be had and are recommended yearly as soon as you turn 60 years old. And there is no cure for HIV, so HIV test after condom less sex, especially if you're single.

You may have heard about acid reflux disease and it's cousin, GERD (gastric esophageal reflux disease). I have had both forms of this disease, and still do. Let me tell you the truth about both gastric ailments from my own experiences. I noticed as of my 27th year of life that when I would drink beer or other alcohol I would start to throw up after a few drinks. I couldn't keep my liquor down no matter what. Things stayed like that for 15 years, but I kept right on drinking. Then one day, I noticed that every time I ate pizza or tomato sauce, I would throw up. Soon, I couldn't eat eggs or milk or meat anymore without regurgitating. Then I couldn't even half swallow my food, and thought I might have stomach or esophageal cancer. I took my regurgitating self to a doctor, and explained my symptoms. I told the doctor that sometimes I even throw up stomach acid and it goes into my mouth and burns. The doctor concluded that I was under the influence of acid reflux disease(improper enzyme balance in the esophagus) and told me to avoid alcohol, tomato sauce products, citrus juice, chocolate, and spearmint/peppermint candy. The doctor advised medication called Prilosec. If you need reflux pills, Prilosec seems to be the cheapest pill, and I found that I don't have to take them every day for relief. I still have trouble swallowing meat and bread even on Prilosec, as my acid reflux has now been converted into GERD. If you have symptoms such as I've experienced you may want to let a doctor look at you. Not taking acid inhibitors like Prilosec or Nexium for what appears to be acid reflux or GERD may result in severe stomach pain, especially if you eat a lot of gas producing food, and even set you up for a case of stomach ulcers and/or esophageal cancer.

Smoking and alcohol are a big part of heart disease and smoking of any type, especially tobacco, marijuana, salvia, or crack cocaine, is really asking for strokes and maybe cancer. Are you really prideful when you give in to drug use just to fit in or relax, even when medical journals constantly warn of terminal, possibly incurable disease from smoking and alcohol use?

Smoking and chewing of tobacco invites over 237 known carcinogens into your internal organs. A man I've been friends with who I knew was a smoker died before his 57th birthday of pancreatic cancer. I've had more than 4 family members die from cancer, and I knew they were smokers. One family member of mine quit smoking for 15 years and still had a brain stroke at 57 and lived partially physically crippled for 13 years before another brain stroke claimed his life. I don't think it's worth it to smoke, and I refuse to.

The people who take up for the cause of medicinal marijuana say they want cancer patients to have the right to use marijuana because it's a cheap pain killer, and cancer patients need to have the right to alleviate pain. I wonder how anyone can say it is empirically sound minded to give a cancer patient marijuana to smoke, when marijuana is 5 times more carcinogenic than tobacco and then claim that that type of marijuana use is medicinal. THC pills derived from pot may be better for alleviating pain and don't have intoxicant effects of smoking pot, and are not more carbon emission from smoke that the Earth doesn't need. Cancer patients should stick with opiates for pain. Doctors say to help try to reduce cancer you should stick with a low saturated fat diet, stay under 256 grams carbohydrates a day, stay under 100 grams sugar per day, and under 24 oz. alcohol/24 hour period.

In 2008 I saw something on a 60 Minutes television show segment where the subject was a drug called Prometa. Prometa is said to be a drug that eliminates the urge to use cocaine, alcohol, and amphetamines. If you suffer under such addictions, you might want to ask your doctor about Prometa. I don't know how much the treatment costs, but it might be something to look into for those seeking an end to overt drug dependence. Most people that used Prometa said it worked for them. 50% of doctors who were asked about Prometa said the drug works, and 50% of doctors who were asked about Prometa said it doesn't work. If you have a cocaine, alcohol, or amphetamine addiction and seek to end your addiction, ask a doctor about Prometa.

I always believe what Alcoholics Anonymous and Narcotics Anonymous says, that if you want to give up drug addictions, the best way to quit is for you to want to quit. You can't really expect to be able to quit drugs unless you really have an authentic desire to quit. In essence, healthy body, healthy mind.

There are some in many societies who just don't fit in with sobriety. There are those in a society who would rather live outside of the corporate entity. They may be called heathens, deviants, and even losers, but the will for them to live by their own standards and not standards decreed by morals and customs of the society they live is strong. Some people will defy humanity, even God in the name of freedom to think and live as they see fit. I'm going to examine some of these people whom you might not know how they can live the way they live, and give my own insight into subcultures said by some to be provocative among mankind. I will show you how I deal with iconoclasm without anxiety. Whether you are conformist or nonconformist to the society you live in, is there an authentically empirical reason for you to live the way you live? Please read further . . .

Chapter 5

WE DON'T WANT TO
BE LIKE YOU

Some people choose iconoclasm as a way of life. Such is the way of members of the Church of Satan, which was founded by the late Anton LaVey.

The Church of Satan has a Satanic bible that was authored by Mr. LaVey, and this Satanic bible instructs it's readers on how to properly worship Satan, and it even includes a section on the Satanic Black Mass, for selling your soul to Satan.

The Satanic church headquarters was located in Fremont, California as of 2011, at which time the leadership of the church was taken over by Mr. LaVey's daughter. The Church of Satan has web pages and info on how you can become a member. One of the main functions of the Church of Satan is to make people question their dependence on orthodox Christian-based religion and to attempt to show Satan as a leader in objective defiance of conformism to Jesus and Jehovah, and many other religions. The Church of Satan has a motto they preach, which is 'there is no god but man.' I have heard tales of promiscuous sex orgies at gatherings of Church of Satan members. Drug use by members of the Church of Satan is considered non Satanic by the present day leader and members of Church of Satan. It costs $200.00 to join the Church of Satan. The Church of Satan web page tells you where to send your money if you want to join them.

The Church of Satan suggests you read a copy of the Satanic bible if you're interested in membership. The Church of Satan also has some rules they go by for people wanting to follow in the way that Church of Satan says is appropriate behavior. Here is a sample of several major rules of the Church of Satan . . . do not kill non human animals unless you are attacked or for food, and when walking in open territory, bother no one. If one bothers you, ask him to stop. If he doesn't, destroy him. Don't tell your troubles to others unless you're sure they want to hear it. Also, don't give opinions or advice unless asked, and don't harm children. Don't complain about anything for which you don't need to subject yourself. And, no sexual advances unless you are given mating signals . . .

I basically agree with the majority of these aforementioned rules, including the part about destroying someone if they refuse to quit bothering you, or you not giving opinions or advice unless asked. But don't let cynicism stifle objectivity.

Perhaps there is gain or profit in helping people, objectively perceived. Honestly,

I don't want to join the Church of Satan, and I don't believe in giving any prestige to Satanists because I feel I can think properly for myself without them.

You might be more inclined to regard the Church of Satan movement as nothing significant if it's not something you care to believe in. You do have a choice.

Apparently there are some people willing to chance the Lake of Fire, and they derive pleasure out of their rebellion against God to the point they don't see any need of conformism to Christianity or anything but Satan, or heathenism.

The Church of Satan members ideas of sacrilege are acts they chose voluntarily, and even if those acts include sodomy(heterosexual or homosexual) I see no reason to hate Satanists. Fear of the occult is irrational and isn't proven natural. You weren't born scared of anything, so why would you let anything fool you out of rational thought? If you are anti empirical enough to have fear, do you really know Satan for you to know if he's anything you need to fear?

If you are anti empirical enough to be angry at people for choosing Satan instead of Jehovah and Jesus, you are irrational and risking punishment in eternal flames.

And what would you have to be angry about if you're on the path to salvation?

Since 1963, the American Atheists Association has pressed for the civil liberties of atheists and the total, absolute separation of religions and humans.

An atheist is said to believe that it is proper for people to love themselves instead of a god. The American Atheist Association says people should love themselves plus their fellow man instead of a god. According to the American Atheists Association, heaven is right here on Earth and it will do people no good to pray to any god because you will get no help from doing such.

Materialism is a concept of the American Atheists that declares that the cosmos is devoid of purpose and there is no supernatural interference in life from any thing similar to the description of a god. I was always told all my life that an atheist believed God was dead, and the American Atheists are saying that God never even existed in the first place. The American Atheists Association collects data and literature on all religions to objectively face enemies without fear.

Know your enemy. With empirical objectivism, I don't fear the opposition.

I believe there is a God, named Jehovah. I also thought that I gave up the ghost once while I was sleeping. How do I know I wasn't dreaming? Well, as soon as I felt myself seemingly awake, I sat up in my bed, and I saw people walking in circles while 8 ft. tall men in white robes were standing around them.

Everything was in black and white; was it the afterlife, people waiting for ascension? The same night I could feel a body in bed with me, and a voice from the body said "I am Lilith", and I could see the body had the same face on it as the face on a picture of a stone bas-relief I had on my wall, which showed the face of Lilith. You can say either I gave up the ghost that night, or was only dreaming. I believe in Jehovah and that Jesus is his son from my observations the night I had what seems like an out of body experience.

There are religious zealots who go to extremes to try to push their religious beliefs on others. Zealots for religion can be into Christianity, or some other religion, and may include all those said to be deities by religious texts.

Zealots may follow a religious creed and assume they can do anything they want, if it's done in the name of religion. These zealot types may insist if others don't follow their ways, they will be damned. Zealots for religion believe in following their bibles verbatim and all other views are heresy. A person who defies science empiricism to find comfort in faith is said to be a religious zealot, as in a person who believes only 2 people were created by God(Jehovah) when all people don't have the same DNA as a brother and sister of a same parent do. Be rational.

I don't really see anything wrong with people wanting religion to be important and the cornerstone of their life. I hope that people will be empirical manner of thought before they assume that everything in the bible is guaranteed factual and beyond questioning. It is said in the King James bible that God says don't be fools. My advice to anyone is no convention without question; that goes for questioning the texts that men call science as well as religious texts. Empiricism is the way I find peace of mind, and properly used, empiricism works for me . . . maybe for you too. And, if you can take the liberty to be Christian against societies that seem tolerant of perfidy, you're not conservative or liberal, but obviously out to do what you consider practical for your attempt to be spared life in the Lake of Fire. I believe all people will receive the Lake of Fire if they are not Christian.

I was always told high school dropouts never make as much money in their lifetime as college/university graduates. I've seen high school dropouts who had dedicated their life to prostitution/drugs and ended up as homosexuals.

Some of these dropouts were having regrets that they didn't do anything to fit in with their society all their life and some were not affording marriages and also didn't think to bother to get a GED certificate. For anyone who is currently unemployed or on general assistance, and has no drug convictions and will work, try to get some type of federal government grant if you have a GED and seek a community college education for some type of medical assistant program.

The United States needs medical technicians, and that's a type of program that doesn't require too much mathematics, if you've had trouble with math in your previous scholastic career. At least that's a way of making $700.00 a week or more so you won't live a life of regrets claiming you never had fun in life or never had money for a car or marriage, like so many people I've heard of who were high school dropouts. Some dropouts I've known that had cars to drive were only getting car insurance paid because of their parents. Some dropouts I know ended up too preoccupied with drugs to keep any type of relationships except with some welfare type, or they just didn't have the education to have skills to pull anyone to sex with except prostitutes. Some of the high school dropouts I know were bisexuals 20 years ago and now they are having regrets because they really wanted to be married and have children, but because they dropped out of high school they didn't have proper social skills and now live in resentment because they had to resort to homosexuality just to have a lover.

I've seen derelict status of many college dropouts who might have wanted some person more educated than a high school dropout type drug addict and don't take to that type of social scene well, but didn't bother to educate themselves enough to fit in with college/university graduates and had to sleep with themselves or prostitutes for not going to school and work. If you don't want to be left out of bourgeois society, get as much education as you can, and bother to work for a living. Don't live to regret what you don't call gain or pleasure.

Punk rockers have been around at least as far back as 1974 and a lot of times they are high school dropouts. A lot of punks use illegal drugs and preach freedom and originality. If you are not true to yourself, a lot of times a punk will consider you a poseur; just a fake. Some punks aren't into illegal drugs and are called straight edge. There are tattoo punks and skateboard punks.

Many punks reject political idealisms and listen to music that reflects anarchy and iconoclasm seeking. Many punks I've talked to were down on capitalism and into socialism. Socialism uses legal tender, and the use of legal tender is known as capitalism. What do punks have as an alternative to concepts of capitalism, to compensate people for work? I truly don't believe that there are too many people working for free, and since all peoples values aren't the same then legal tender (capitalism) seems like empiricism in government. Many punks are into Satanism, yet some of them want government to continue to support welfare checks(Christianity). Many punks preach down with racism and say they stand for racial equality but I never see many of them as race mixers;

I see more race mixing among the so called squares at the university campus, while I don't see many punk types at any colleges. If I do see punks at college or university, they are rather snot nose if I didn't dress clothes of a punk.

The punks that are saying people are 'conservatives' are usually reserving their time of the day for only punk types, which seems like just another collectivist scheme of anti objectivists not seeking evolution of human species over cynicism and tunnel vision. If I've got to wear clothes, then the clothes I choose will not be a stereotype of some herd minded, whether that herd be punk or some other clique. As far as scenes of industrial punk music go, what is avant-garde about wearing grandmas sweater or shopping at the Goodwill store for hand-me-downs?

In other words, what is avant-garde about atavistic style, or rather, imitating styles of your grandparents? While there may be nothing modern, atavistic is contrary to seeking the primordial. Punk values aren't always empirical judgment.

Republicans are sometimes seen as catering only to moneyed people. I've heard republicans cry that socialism is treasonous, and about President Obama trying to turn the U.S. into a socialist government. Social security and welfare are socialism, and republicans didn't seem to complain about those socialism minded programs until President Obama took office. Not only are Social Security and welfare socialism, but SSA/SSI/welfare are actually also Christianity which republicans claim they are for, but some republicans suggest ending SSA/SSI. Some republicans seem to snob Christianity like they are afraid they and their supporters will starve to death. If an SSI/SSA/welfare recipient all of a sudden started working a job, they'd still eat the same amount of food they were eating when they were unemployed. Empirically, you can be Christian and give money to feed people, but you may not want to or afford to give money.

Looks like some republicans complaints are about people that don't work getting more money than republicans think they should. Republicans haven't proven all welfare/SSI recipients are on illegal drugs. President Clinton on NBC television said republicans have no problem supporting tax increases for war movements, but tax increases to fund programs for the unemployed, tax increases far less than taxes spent on war movements, republicans have shown much opposition to.

I will support an empirical candidate for congress and president of the U.S.A., and not depend on voting along party lines, even in times of food and shelter shortages. Yes, some people on SSI/welfare have job skills, but don't get hired for work. I hope you will pick empiricism, not republicans or democrats.

The topic of homosexuality is in the news constantly. It is said that most U.S. adults favor same-sex marriages. There is a belief system about gays: most religions say homosexuality is an abomination and immoral. A lot of people say that they expect change from gays, and that gays can and must change their sexual orientation and become heterosexuals. Some people expect homosexuals to be celibate if they cannot change their ways. A belief among some is that same sex marriage is better than promiscuous sex lifestyles. There are movements for gay people to receive equal rights in many societies of the Earth, and these movements say that homophobia is an 'evil'. I do not believe in practicing homosexuality with anyone in this or any universe. However, I don't really see a need to hate gay people. As hatred is irrational, if you are just plain physically repulsed by gay people, you might be so because of what bibles say. If bibles are the reason for your being sickened by gay people, you might want to seek empiricism and consider that if you feel gays are inferior, what do you have to do with someone else's business? God will deal with every person individually, including you. Is your slate clean of transgression against God? According to the book of Numbers, people that don't race mix are just as sinful as homosexuals are said to be. The book of James says if you did one sin, you did them all.

Consider that the next time you cry about homosexuals, or anyone's choice not to stick with morals of Christian and Muslim bibles.

Recreational drug users, from my experience, are usually using drugs that many governments say are not to be used without prescription by doctors, or drugs that are not regulated by the FDA and DEA and are found to be offensive by police and other government bureaucrat types for people to use illegally.

Some people use their drugs to relieve themselves of what they say are pressures they may or may not experience from work or other social settings they may claim are uncomfortable. I truly believe that if you use drugs outside of aspirins and drug use in accordance with a doctors prescription you may be in need of some self-esteem. Even if you claim your drug use is done just to relax, does it look like people have pride when their use of drugs turns abusive and they never seem to enjoy life or anything they get without some type of drug use?

Test yourself and see if you can curb your appetite for drugs without pain.

If you have discomfort from withdrawal from drugs, you're possibly addicted.

Intravenous amphetamine and cocaine can lead to brain stroke and heart disease, and drugs used intravenously may also increase the risk of hepatitis A, B, and C, and also may introduce you to flesh eating bacteria

(Clostridium Perfrengens) and HIV. Some balloons of heroin coming from Mexico may even be 90% pure dope instead of the usual weak stuff most people get when they buy heroin and makes it easier for you to accidentally overdose and die. Are you really that desperate to get high, like society was that bad that you couldn't continue to function day to day without some type of intoxicant? Maybe some people get as much pleasure from drugs as they do from sex. I'm happy with being sober, and glad for the simple pleasure of food, drink and the existence, and don't need to be stoned because I've got peace of mind from being rational for the practical.

Race mixers are in many societies and don't see to stay with their own race/subspecies and are sometimes discriminated against by irrational people who claim that they are proud because they want to keep races segregated and their race pure of race characteristics of other races lips, nose, hair, teeth, and skin.

What is pride about offended and physically nauseated by people race mixing or the existence of mixed breed people on this Earth? It doesn't look in this day and time that race mixing is the downfall of medical prowess or chemical and electrical engineering/math skills in the U.S.A. or Europe. It doesn't look like race mixing will guarantee a increase in crime, and hybrids are said to be more resistant to disease than pure bloods, provided the hybrid doesn't go out of their way to smoke and overuse alcohol. If you say Negro races are more prone to crime than Whites, is it because Negroes are genetically inferior, or because Negroes are not even getting jobs away from Caucasian race supremacists as much as Whites and are wanting more food and goods than what they get?

Anti race mixing is the refusal to give birth with races different than yours and the same thing as genocide of another human race species, a crime against God.

Genocide is not seen as a position of leadership, as the quality of objectivist egalitarianism is said by texts at universities to be a constituent of those intellectually preponderance in correct government than some cynic who plots downfall of every race different from their own, or of their own that race mix, like that proves empiricism of thought instead of pride less irrational sophisms.

Is there a reason to keep race segregation alive, as if you were so inadequate at social skills and illiterate enough to need for there to be pure races to continue to exist, as if you can guarantee that leaving races different than you out of the job pool will make it so you have heterosexual sex prowess with your own kind, or are 100% savvy at empirical method of thought to the point that your job is secure? I want to marry a person that is an empiricist mind and also egalitarian no matter what race they are, instead of crass illiterates that make racism their claim to charisma and intellectual challenge to a 12 year old.

Race mixing is obviously not the downfall of empiricism, and empiricism isn't comprehensible by everyone of the White race, since their are plenty of White race students taking entrance exams at American colleges that don't score as high in test scores percentages as much as Oriental and Hindi students test scores.

If Negro students aren't empirical in math for engineer degrees, and you cared for Western civilization as White supremacists say they do, then why would you tolerate illiteracy in math among Negroes? I see that tolerance as anti Western civilization, anti White races, and anti whoever stands for upkeep of Western civilization, the blueprint and constituents of which are 90% in the name of a white race. For any Negro races crying uncle tom, most of them one way or another have made White race idols a part of their value system . . . baseball, football, basketball, White race holidays, television/electronics, school/English language, White man's religions (including Satanism/Tarot), perm hair relaxers, weave wigs, European and American clothes styles. While many Americans may preach race segregation, China and India are dominating America in industry, and seemingly are seeking to own America. I want rationality for all humans.

The National Socialist White Peoples Party, which is also sometimes called the American Nazi Party, was started in the 1960's by George Lincoln Rockwell. The American Nazis believe in racial segregation and for people to stay with their own race, and are especially opposed to intermarriage between different races. The American Nazis say that animals don't race mix, so why should White people race mix? American Nazis, as well as history books, say the founding fathers of America were slave owners. Some Nazis say Negroes are only 3/5 human. American Nazis claim that the money interests of Israel are put before the interests of the gentiles and small Jews of America by American government. Most American Nazis want one White race nation, and claim that their motto is 'our race is our nation'. The White Peoples Party says White women of child bearing age only compromise about 3% of the Earth's population.

Adolf Hitler, Chancellor of Nazi Germany, is admired by the White Peoples Party, and these Nazis like to wear swastikas, a sign of White race pride like in the days of Hitler's rule. I wonder if American Nazis knew that Hitler called his Japanese partners in WWII physically and intellectually superior to white races in Great Britain. Hitler said blue eyed blonds were superior to non white Japanese races. I believe Great Britain has also birthed blue eyed blonds.

I've noticed that many skinheads calling themselves Nazis are of part Jewish race descent, but I don't believe those Jews are American Nazi Party members.

Some Nazis say communism is a Jewish concept, but Israel isn't communist.

What do you suppose the reason is that the American Nazis are so opposed to the Jew race? If they believe in the King James bible, they wouldn't be crying about Jews since Jews, as well as Greeks and Palestinians, wrote the Judeo-

Christian bible, and hatred of Jews and race mixers is contradictory to Christ Jesus. The American Nazis ought to be glad they live in America, which was founded by White Jews. And just how is American government interest in Israel detrimental to the success of American government? If American government is helping keep Israel richer than the so called small Jew and gentiles, why are people who have no political ties the majority of what gets to live life in Hollywood? Who's stopping the anti Jew race bigots from working to make it in Hollywood, so they can be as moneyed as Jews and gentiles in Hollywood?

It looks like Jews in Hollywood are hiring non Whites, and also White gentiles.

Are the Negroes stopping the White supremacists of the U.S.A. from getting an education so White supremacists can get $1,500.00 a week pay longer than 35 years of their life, like those Whites that make that much money and aren't openly crying race bigotry? A lot of Negroes are stopping themselves with crack addictions/drug addictions from $1,500.00 a week pay checks, and the drug court and jails are full of them. That doesn't make all Negroes drug addicts, or prove none of them capable of empirical leadership of American government, or guaranteed the enemy of the White race. If White races are interested in being supremacy, they might try to train themselves and their children to be mechanical/ civil/ electrical/chemical engineers and to be able to compete with engineers in Germany, Japan, India, China, and Korea, as well as learn to be medical doctors and empirical intellect superior to all men in the Earth/universe, including all of the White race that exists. And they should want the same for all individuals of any race of men. Be empirically objective for rationally practical.

There is a movement in the U.S.A. called Sovereign Citizens that doesn't respect the U.S. president or the IRS. Some of this movement are armed and will kill for their freedom to live outside control by U.S. police.

All I can say about that is that there is a word called vigilante, and some will take that word serious. I do respect the police and the military of the U.S.A.

I am a U.S. military veteran who supports all U.S. presidents past and up to present except Woodrow Wilson (who was in the KKK). Our U.S. military serves all that live in the U.S.A., including Sovereign Citizens groups as well.

Some anti abortionists have taken to violence and murder against physicians who perform abortions. These individuals say they act on the word of God. Well, the book of Luke in Christian bibles says thou shall not kill(chp. 18 verse 20), and love your enemies and do good to those that hate you(chp. 6 verse 27); judge not and ye shall not be judged(chp 6 verse 37) . . . be afraid not of them that kill the body(chp 12 verse 4) . . . fear him which after he hath killed hath power to cast into Hell(chp 12 verse 5). It doesn't look morally correct to kill doctors that perform abortions. And if anti abortionists don't race mix that's genocide, which is also murder, if anti abortionists want to get technical.

Even though abortion is murder, murdering abortionists is the same Lake of Fire.

I don't believe you need to fear God, but the Lake is said to be much pain.

The subcultures I've just described here are a real part of our world. As these subcultures differ in views from me, I can coincide with them. I don't have any problems dealing with people different than me, and I hope you will use empirical, rational thought in dealing with those different than you. 'If you noticed, I have shown how what some people say is provocative about subcultures I have analyzed as nothing more than ideals that aren't altogether empirically rational ideals. Now, how will what is seen as anti empirical continue to be of some type of contingency for you or anyone in your quest for relief from anxiety?

Some of my previous descriptions of subcultures have been about people that are into overt racism. I have seen people of all races commit racism. I will now continue to attempt to justify my claim that racism is anti empirical and degenerate to effectual government/educational process. I want a world of rational thinking people . . . for mental utopia.

Chapter 6

RACISM

Now I will explain how racism is anti empirical and degenerate to effectual government/educational process. Some people think racism is necessary, and are gung ho about the perpetuation of racist ideology. If you are racist against some others of the Earth, was your racism derived from empirical methods for racism to be your only option when dealing with other races? Before I continue to assess whether racism is made obsolete by the empirical or not, I would like to present to you my findings on the subject of Darwinism versus Creationism . . .

Newsweek magazine in 2006 reported that some scientists believe that all humans are genetically related to chimpanzees and that fossils found in Ethiopia, Africa were of human-like/monkey-like species and are 300,000 years old. Now when you do DNA testing to find your ancestors, the test results do not show you to be related to the whole human race, but only some of them. So it seems that many humans didn't come from chimpanzees or apes, if any did. One of my girlfriends has a green birthmark on her left foot, and she said it was the mark of a pure blood Irish race. Hebrew religion says Adam, who is said to be the first man on Earth, was made out of dirt. Hebrew religion didn't say the early Jew races of 3000 years ago had green birthmarks on their feet. Does any race have that green birthmark on their feet except for the Irish? Hebrew Union College in Cincinnati, Ohio says in their libraries that Eve, the supposed first woman on Earth, was an Ethiopian. If DNA testing doesn't show all people related to each other, and my girlfriends green birthmark is particular to the Irish race only, then Adam and Eve aren't the parents of all humanity. It looks more like all races have groups of primordial parents not of Adam and Eve. If DNA tests can prove you are the same relatives of your biological parents, sisters, and brothers, and can tell if your seed is that of a rapist or not, then what guarantee is there that all people came from the same parentage, or monkeys, or Africa? Fossils over 300,000 years old have turned up in Germany and France in the past 32 years. Were those fossils ever said to be monkey-like? Not to my knowledge. Were those fossils genetically similar to Ethiopian fossils scientists said they have found recently? I haven't heard any such findings at all. Are any fossils that are said to be coming out of Africa tested to see if DNA of these fossils are a match with DNA of races different than people of Ethiopia? Fossils found in Africa may be of just some more highly developed monkey, but not all the way human. My biology teacher at University of Cincinnati in 1982 said that humans were also genetically related to pigs and earthworms. I don't know how true that is, but I'm thinking God must have started thinking up humans at the same time as monkeys and the human and monkey species are two separate entities. Again, if the fossils found in Ethiopia show all humans to be related to monkeys, then how come DNA testing for humans to find their human relatives is able to be done, instead of the DNA test results showing you to be related to anyone and everyone, as if humans were all related by all of them being supposedly related to monkeys? I have no sure proof that all humans are actually related to monkeys. How is Negro ancestry, found by DNA testing, different among Negroes if all Negroes came from monkeys?

It takes pride to excel in effectual government/educational process. It also takes pride to do as you see is empirically sound minded. Just how does doing the same behaviors all the time, all your life, guaranteed sound like pride? You might try what's empirical for the practical, not live the life of a puppet. How does doing what is different than usual guaranteed loss of pride? If you have pride instead of cowardice or presumption, presumptions being sophisms, you wouldn't need to stick with living what you were told to do, and would be able to do what you feel like. You should be rational for practical in thought, instead of a victim of someone who couldn't prove that values different than their values are irrational. Doing what people tell you to do when there's really no profit from it and no guaranteed pride from compliance to something you're not comfortable with is the masochistic self victimization of yourself.

Why are some people victimized by different races doing as they please? Surely humans can be more rational than victims. How can you let race of people different than you tick you off if you claim to be of rational thought? White race Greek philosophy values rational thought. So if rational thought is attractive and what's said to make men respectable and of empirical judgment, why emotions of anger and resentment against different races? That is not what White men of the U.S.A. derive their systems of government and education from.

I've heard men say they hated races different than them just because of racial traits. Is that rational thought? Dogs, cats, and monkeys are different races than humans, but who hates dogs, cats, and monkeys? Prove all of your race is guaranteed your friend when you decide to turn against someone because of their race. I say be objective and try investigating sex with all races.

I heard on the radio that pure blood races were less disease resistant than mixed breed people. Is it the end of evolution in mechanical/electrical engineering and medicine because of the end of pure blood people on this Earth? So far, race mixing on this Earth hasn't stopped society from producing medical breakthroughs in cancer research. Actually, the U.S.A. has seen an increase in Negroes in medical and engineering professions from increased ambition due to desegregation in the 70's. That's more desirable than inertia.

What do you need to keep pure blood races on the Earth for? Pride is said to come from accomplishment. Do all of your race live to lead government? You can say your race looks better than all other races, but all of your race doesn't guaranteed agree with that concept. You can say your race is biologically and genetically superior to all other races, but hemolysins (bacteria that destroy red blood cells) and leukocydins (bacteria that destroy white blood cells) are able to destroy all human races, although mixed breeds are said to be more disease resistant than pure blood races.

You cant miss what you can't measure . . . if you've never had love or sex before, why would you hurt from lack of it? Is it rational minded to hate other people, other races, because you didn't get love? No, it's not. And most people I've heard that say they hurt from lack of love and hate it to see race mixers . . . do you think what they were turned down by for love was guaranteed a race mixer for them to irrationally take hatred to other races, like they or any of us are guaranteed sexually and intellectually satisfactory to any and all of our own race?

You weren't born racist, and to say racism is rational thought is absurd. If you can't prove all White race thought is rationally practical for you, or that Negroes need to value everything White society values, then how can you prove Negroes are intellectually inferior to Whites? Do all White races value or need to value everything Whites say is desirable, for Negroes to lick up on everything a White race person says is of importance? When people constantly beg you for respect and patronage and they have no tangible practical value in your life, they don't seem to me to have pride, no matter how racist, sexist, or lucrative they seem. So much for race supremacists. Collectivist ideals like race bigotry are not catering to nurturing self-esteem. How can you let a race represent you, as an individual, like you can somehow guarantee conquer chemistry and physics with racism instead of objectivism? Racism in my opinion is no more a mask to try to hide how substandard you are for pride in yourself. Pride through racism styles doesn't prove you have worth to society as a whole, or anyone that's bourgeois or leadership position. What I'm telling you here needs to be analyzed by every student in the Earth, as a defense against fascists/racists and a go ahead to show some pride in yourself and quit trying to victimize people because of race, like you want to make it on your own strengths instead of stink up our world with the irrational and the absurd. If you're a loser that has regrets about something, as intelligent as people usually are, do you think you can hide it that you're a resentful loser to be thinking that racism will keep people from seeing resentment and hearing that you're a loser, a cynical, condescending loser?

Hopefully I've shown how degenerate racism is to science/government; no one is proving to me that the U.S.A. is run on racism, or only by racists. As successful as the U.S.A. is in running government, if the U.S.A. was a racist government, how do you explain all the over $100,000.00 a year people of all races I've seen in the U.S.A? Who stopped you from $100,000.00 cash a year? Was it the other races? Negroes that say they are short changed by Whites out of money over 100 grand a year aren't proving they're disadvantaged. Do Negroes without 2/3 grand a week prove all of the White races were out to stop them? Some Negroes in the music industry in Los Angeles in 1992 said that if you don't work, you don't eat . . .

Cynics in racism don't seem to be presenting an argument that breaks peoples will to succeed, no matter what their race. Are you going to let the absurdity of racism control your happiness?

Racism is a distraction from empirical, rational thought. It seems like the leaders of America haven't let racism interfere with government. People usually live a comfortable life here in America. Why let the irrational take away from efforts to get what you want out of life, instead of delving in the ludicrous at the whim of race bigots? Racism is seen by me as degenerate to not only America, but the Earth.

Where do people get the ridiculous idea that if someone is enemy with them, that all members of the race of their enemy are out to destroy them, or are also the enemy of them? Government seems to function in an objective manner, and racists making enemies of all of the race of their enemies are only operating on generalizations, which are sophist and irrational. Who wants to do school/work with bigots and trust their valuables or life with people who are irrational, absurd, and not sound empirical thought? American technology didn't get to the level it is today from irrational thought and behavior.

I have heard some Negroes and Whites telling Negroes to lick uncle tom to White people. These people requesting that Negroes lick uncle tom say it's to be done for any and all Whites, as if a White that's a high school dropout or on welfare is the same thing as a Negro, Asian, or White chemical engineer that works, who really couldn't prove with any sort of chemical equation that Negro people need to lick uncle tom to any White to be able to think in an empirical manner of thought, or figure out what's most practical for their tastes to involve themselves with. I don't see anything rational about Negro people licking uncle tom to any White race, including White engineers and chemists. If I was hated for not licking uncle tom, I'd rather be hated if it meant I was empirical and proud than cringing as a coward. Uncle toms go out of their way to snob Negroes where I come from, and don't seem to think high enough to seek out effectual leaders of all races instead living life pride less and bowing to race like useless, pride less jerks who couldn't have self-esteem unless they had someone to turn their nose up to with racism, to give them some kind of hope of pride. Uncle Negroes are usually the joke of Negroes with prestige from Whites and that don't kiss White ass, and uncles may let Whites do all the governing of people without question.

I have fallen in love with people of all races, and just because you love someone of a different race than yours, it doesn't seem rational to hate your own race or all races different than the race of the one you love. What is pride about hate, letting someone piss you off when your peace of mind is more important than somebody's decision that wasn't in league with your choices in life? And most people can see whether you're Negro or White, so if you've got pride then you don't need to push race and religion down other peoples throat in pride less collectivism used as an excuse for prestige.

Adult dogs and cats are usually seen as only rational as 3 year old humans. But most dogs and cats are not seemingly humiliated by having Negroes for family. If adult humans are humiliated by having Negroes for their family, doesn't that look more ridiculous and irrational than most cats and dogs? Aren't all race bigots who don't want their family to race mix looking more irrational than most dogs and cats who aren't thought of as rational as adult humans? And if racism comes from pride, then why would you let the so called inferior race mixer destroy your happiness if you had true pride? Rational thought by me that's proven to be rational with empirical measurement gives me pride. Whereas hate is seen as irrational, then so is racism irrational. Thus, racism appears to look obsolete to empirical, rational thought.

Governmental/educational process cares for bourgeoisie made, not the perpetuation of race bigots no more rational than elementary school children. America, and the world needs evolution in technology from the minds of men and women of all races. I hope what I write here will be of some use to all people of the world. Peace on Earth . . . for mental utopia. Please continue to read . . .

Chapter 7

RELIGION

Some who seek mental utopia turn to religion. I have my own personal thoughts on religion, and I'd like to share these thoughts with you. My interpretation of religion is done as empirically as possible. Here are some of my views on religions of the world, especially Judeo-Christian religion . . .

I believe that Jehovah and Jesus are the only Gods that can redeem people from eternal punishment. Allah is said to be the god of Muslims, but I truly don't believe Allah will keep us from the Lake of Fire, the ever lasting flames prepared by Jehovah. I believe Jehovah created man in his image and man did not come from monkeys. If man came from monkeys, DNA testing of man would reveal all humans to be related to all other humans if all humans are related to monkeys. I have a soul and it came out of my body several times in my life, so I also believe in life after death. I don't even believe we can die unless we are obliterated, so it really won't do any good to commit suicide, especially since suicide is said to be sacrilege by Judeo-Christian religion, so you'd just be in for more punishment than before you attempted to commit suicide if you suicide.

I believe of all the different books in the King James bible of Judeo-Christian religion, the most important ones for your salvation from punishment are Exodus, Numbers, Luke, Corinthians, and James. The book of James explains how if you did one sin, you did them all, which is something for you who are putting down murderers and rapists, but are racists, sodomites, or liars yourselves. I believe in the book of Exodus you will find the Ten Commandments of Jehovah, which are his laws that man is to live by for salvation purposes.

The Ten Commandments are as follows . . . you are to honor your mother and father, you shall not steal, you shall not covet your neighbors wife or goods, you shall not kill, you should remember the Sabbath day and keep it holy, you should not bear false witness, you should not use God's name in vain, you do not commit adultery, you should have no graven images before you, and you should not have another god instead of Jehovah and Jesus. If you're vigilante for your own laws you devised, then you may not look at the Ten Commandments as useful. Jesus, son of Jehovah, said to keep the Ten Commandments holy.

Judeo-Christian religion says that all that believe in Jesus will be saved from eternally punished in the Lake of Fire. But those that are marked with the Mark of the Beast are never saved from burning in eternal flames of the Lake of Fire, even if they believe in Jesus as God. Once you have the Mark of the Beast, you may then at that point know Jesus is God, but it's too late to be sparred the Lake of Fire by then. Jews are not exempt from God's judgment, and can receive the Mark of the Beast also. The son of Adam named Cain received the Mark of the Beast, and he was Jewish.

One thing I cannot understand is how people think that Satan is the root of all 'evil'. Satan is said to be a scapegoat; if you decide to transgress against Jesus, you can't blame Satan for your decisions without God punishing you for your sins, not Satan. Satan will only pay for whatever transgression he has done, not any sins you decided to commit. I truly doubt Satan tells anyone to do anything against God or humans, outside of trying to turn Job against Jehovah.

I believe all who do not obey Jesus and speak it that Jesus is the most important God and savior of mankind will be burned in the Lake of Fire.

The Judeo-Christian bible book of Proverbs has many mentions of the word wisdom. The word wisdom is similar to the word logic. Logic is what is said to be, like wisdom, doing what's practical. But all mans ideas of what's practical aren't the same as every mans idea of practical, so how do the words wisdom and logic describe reality? All I can say about the word wisdom in Proverbs is that whoever wrote Proverbs must think it's highly practical to obey Jehovah.

If you don't know where your next meal or shelter is coming from, then how is there such a thing as greed? Some religions warn about greed for the temporal, and how it is sin. In the Song of Solomon (Judeo-Christian bibles) King Solomon was richer than anyone in Israel, but no one ever called his large amounts of property and gold foolish, at least not to my knowledge. Perhaps if you give a percentage of your monies to the people with far less than you, that will make up for being a millionaire. I don't know. I wouldn't turn down the life of a millionaire. You be the judge. God will judge you too.

The Judeo-Christian book of Genesis says Noah's sons Shem, Ham, and Japeth are the fathers of all the people on the Earth. DNA tests will tell you that all people didn't come from monkeys or the same blood line. It looks like Moses, writer of the Torah (1st 5 books of Judeo-Christian bibles), did some exaggerating in his testament. From my seeing pure blood race characteristics, I believe all races have groups of primordial pure blood race parents.

From my studies of Judeo-Christian religion, I believe once you repent you should not continue to transgress against God. God doesn't trust perfidy, and asking for his forgiveness after every new sin will not work, and you will burn in the Lake of Fire for your flippancy.

Just like the preacher at the gospel mission church said to me, all the rituals of Christian churches or any church don't have any importance. Either you believe that Jesus saves those that are not marked with the Beast number on their right palm and except him as God and obey him completely or you will live in the Lake of Fire. All church rituals are useless if you are marked with the Beast number. And the gospel mission told me that the Lake of Fire isn't in Hell; Hell is where Satan lives, and where all people go including those that are saved in Christ, and all people stay in until Metatron, one of God's angels, takes the race of humans to the Judgment. The Lake of Fire is said to be millions of miles away from God's heaven and the Hell (Purgatory).

There seems to be nothing wrong with being anti religious rituals at life, as long as you do what Jesus says if you want to live with him.

When your soul leaves the body, it doesn't hurt at all, and you don't need to breathe anymore. There is no feeling of suffocation in giving up the ghost.

Why would you think Satan has such a thing as an alter of sacrifice? Why would there be an alter of sacrifice when you are already a ghost in Hell? Do you prove Satan has power to disintegrate a ghost? If there's a Mark of the Beast, then you get to live to see Judgment. Then Metatron will take you and all of us to Judgment (according to the Hebrew text called the Golden Dawn). The King James bible says the soul is eternal, and so is the Lake of Fire. If that's true, do you think Satan has power to dismember you? If the Lake was made for Satan, then why would Satan ever bother to dismember or obliterate people, because then he would just be asking for more punishment than what Jesus plans on giving him. Do you think Satan will take that kind of chance? From that assessment, possibly Satan isn't the one that puts the Mark on people. The Hebrews said Satan was a murderer because he and Baal sent people off this Earth in the Middle East in the years after Adam and Lilith. But Satan and Baal and Lilith were making catalepsy of Jews, and I don't know if they were hostile to other races. The Satanic bible says Satan is your friend, and has parties for you. The Judeo-Christian book of Genesis also has some kind of statement in it, says Jack Chick bible comic books, that Satan is waiting to meet you in Hell and wants to make love to you.

Why does a rock group named Christian Death think that Christians need to be killed? Some Christian church goers said they want me saved from the Lake, and gave me money when I was homeless. Christians, or perhaps Samaritans, run homeless shelters and soup kitchens for the out on the street types. Can the rock group Christian Death prove that Christians want to see homosexuals killed? Or murderers on death row killed?

You can say love the enemy, but you still are told to defend yourself from attack, sexual or other type . . . the true Christian will not defend itself, and may even opt to be destroyed and let God take responsibility for the punishment of those out to beat the Christian.

Before you sacrilege, you might want to consider that God doesn't have to forgive you, so don't expect forgiveness for any sin even if Jesus said to pray if you were wanting to repent. Don't take that statement as cynicism, but as a warning for your soul.

What do you do if your parents preach irrational racist hatred against others, to the point of segregation and death wishes on other races? Well, all members of the racial group your parents are against are not responsible for your and your parents problems. If you are of rational mind or a Christian, or both, you will reject your parents ways of sacrilege even if they turn against you, as it is said better to save your soul than to wallow in what God says is filth.

How can you be pro-life and then oppose race mixing? And, how can you dictate to a pregnant woman that she can't get an abortion if she decides to? If God says don't kill, then you shouldn't kill unless you feel it's right. If people feel that abortion is right for them, the responsibility of the act is not something anyone has to answer for but the woman having an abortion. You only pay for what you have transgressed, not anyone else's abortions, rapes, homosexuality, homicides, suicides, etc.

If right wing groups support the death penalty but are anti abortion, they are contradictory to the Judeo-Christian bibles, which say no to all death. Jesus said to turn the other cheek against your enemies, if you claim to be Christian.

The King James bible is the correct bible for Christians. Any bible other than the King James bible is the wrong bible, and any religion that isn't Christian is the wrong religion for those that want to be saved from the Lake of Fire. Tell that to the world, and all mans posterity. There are only two true religions . . . you can choose Satan, or you can choose Jesus. If you don't choose Jesus you will receive nothing but punishment, said to be painful eternally.

You can take the religions of the world, but the God doesn't need your religion. All he needs is your respect, and the same respect given to him given to all the people of the Earth. Empiricism will be useful in dealing with peoples negative emotions.

I used to be a mentally disturbed fellow until I took an empirical approach to external to my brain. I have a system of thinking of which you have sampled here in some of the text I've written so far. I'd like to continue to share my system for dealing with negative, irritating thoughts that make for mental discomfort. One of the biggest problems we face today is the number of people who are severely depressed. I used to be one of them. Now, I'm cured, and I've been cured for over 20 years. Let me show you how I cured myself from depression, and ascended to great heights of mental utopia.

Chapter 8

STEPS TO CURE DEPRESSION

I have a 12 point plan for beating depression that worked so well I managed to throw away anti-depression medications I used to take. I'm going to describe some of my plan for you here . . . for mental utopia.

I first had to stop and think about some of the causes of my depression. I came to realize that I had a fear of being a loser. When I couldn't get my way, I had a feeling I wasn't intelligent enough for people I couldn't control. That feeling deprived me of pride. I became fearful that I was inadequate intellectually. Fear made me tired and depressed. At the time I couldn't feel good without drugs, and I didn't realize it took more than sex acts to have pride. Other peoples pride less ness to have to cling to stereotypes and sophisms that many of my society said was proper behavior is what I believe I had bought.

One day I began to notice that I was putting more emphasis on pleasing others egos than pleasing my own ego. From then on I chose to decide for myself what was a loser behavior. Nihilism told me I didn't need to care about other peoples selfish ends unless I could gain profit from such. While there is no guarantee that anything I pursue will permanently free me of regret, I chose the one thing that freed me of regret in the instant . . . I decided that empiricism thought would tell me what was practical for me, not someone else that was not proven interested in my benefit. At that point there was no more fear from me to be called a failure in life because my values were put before all others in importance. At that point, you couldn't prove your value to me for you to be able to ridicule me, and I also considered enemies perfidy. Then I lost much irrational fear.

One of my next goals in pursuit of freedom from depression was to figure out how to be satisfied when I didn't get what I wanted. If supposed to get certain things you may want in life existed, I'll be surprised. Consider this: if you are not ever told of a things existence, then how will it be of any consequence if you don't ever get to 'have' that object, for you to think you really need what the marketplace says is good for you? Prove that because humanity says they can't live without a person or thing that they can't, for you to feel like you're obligated to compliment someone's ego by giving value to things that are not even proven to make your food more nutritious, or your life any less stressful. My pride increased through empiricism. You can't really guarantee you'll have a roof over your head all your life, or enough food. Don't you want to instill some pride in yourself in lean times? Or period? And why delude yourself that you'd be happier with more money if you are still resentful of other people's success? More than enough money may be good for food and shelter, but you may have heard money can't guaranteed buy happiness.

I took a look at some things my society said was good, and claimed that I'd be missing out on something wonderful if I didn't conform to what some said was essential for happiness. Not having things my society said were essential to happiness didn't take away from my enjoyment of food and rest, and all I could think of those that said I was missing out of fun by not buying into my society's idols was that they look like fools. People caring to lick some of my society's idols hurt when nobody shared their enthusiasm for idols I dismissed as trivial, insignificant, and obsolete. Can you prove there's a reason for the existence of humanity for you to put more importance on other peoples values than what serves your purposes?

My next step to cure depression is for me to look at myself as someone who has to be intellectual preponderance over all others, so as not to be weak enough to worship the temporal, instead of strong in rational thought that shows success in pride. Let no man be your superior in empirical assessment of the external to your autonomy, your own physiology. If people correctly show preponderance to your intellect, don't take offense to it out of irrational forms of emotionalism, but thank yourself that your error in thought was detected and rejoice that you have found a higher intellect, as long as that intellect is empirically sound and is ergonomically superior to show gain of your values. There was a sentiment in the U.S.A. in the 20th century that claimed life is a burden, as if people were guaranteed going to suffer somehow. Empiricism makes that type of cynical sophism an obsolete, irrational claim, and degenerate to the cause of boosting peoples morale and work ethic. We don't really need neutering of idealisms when none can guarantee anything perfect. As idealism is what made the blueprint for much technology we witness today, why be docile and depend on rigid orthodoxy to be effectual permanently, and not question life for more convenience for humanity? Just as life on Earth seems temporary, you also really don't have to let peoples idiosyncrasies or technology trample your success and peace of mind.

Some of my process for ridding myself of depression is to consider that I might have to work until I die. If you or I lived in the A.D. 1500's, we might have had to work 10 to 12 hours a day, six days a week. If you have to work, try to get used to it. Hard is all in our mind. No matter what the physical strain is, work is something I believe shouldn't infuriate anyone, no matter what. Now, how do you guarantee beat depression so you can want to work if you're irrational enough to need illegal drugs, or meds from doctors for irrationality? I noticed that some people who were on SSI mental disability were spending their checks on drug parties. I've seen SSI recipients party their whole SSI check and even prey on people with nothing but dole checks for money for some more drugs, and a lot of times these SSI users of illegal drugs are not known to be mentally competent to achieve any type of employment skills, if they even tried. Work freed my mind from depression, as did practicing empirical, rational styles of thought that I don't believe is in the capacity of many illegal drug users. Some people that told me they hear voices can and do work jobs easily. Some people think only those that work should have the right to use recreational drugs. I would want people that I had to work with to be sober while they were on the job site, as I think it would really help reduce accidents. Every SSI recipient for mental claims should at least try to educate themselves beyond high school, and I also believe if they feel they can work then they should, and even try to do college attendance for better work skills and pay. SSI mental claims are usually told to take meds. U.S. government used to test SSI mental check recipients to see if they took their medications up until 1998. U.S. government should reinstate that test, as I feel taxpayers deserve that much. SSI mental claims are usually told by doctors not to mix meds with illegal drugs and alcohol. SSI recipients should be aware that working jobs and getting job skills is asked of them more and more by the Social Security administration. You don't want to be on drugs of any type at work, including psychotropic meds. SSI recipients might want to wean themselves off meds and try work.

I was never into lying to myself and saying I was what people wanted to be involved with after 1979. After I learned how to come by self-esteem, I didn't need to force myself on people like a cat or a dog. Then it was never necessary to be angry when people had differences in opinion than mine, or different tastes in clothes or music, like some animals that are begging to be important. Why would you think you need to be cared about by people that have no use for you, as if you were a mental birth defect? Did you prove that your infatuation with people who don't obviously need you to live was profit? Did you ever stop and think that all people don't think you're sexually attractive? Do you have some type of proof that you are sexual to anyone? Don't you realize if somebody wanted to have sex, they can go to a prostitute instead of you? You are possibly not even considered interesting or sexual by 90% of the Earth. I feel if someone had to prove themselves greatness to people when they are obviously not worth the time of whoever they're trying to brainwash into giving them prestige, such a jerk couldn't be much use to anyone that had more ego than a 7 year old. Dying attempting to make heroes or victims out of those that deprive you of ego makes you look like a real fool, and even a victim yourself. I don't have any heroes. Did it ever occur to you that you are not guaranteed anyone's hero, and had no reason to think you were, especially if you're castrated out of who you pray on for sex and money and friends and obedience for longer than 25 years? When I refused to lie to myself, I was grateful, and have bragged about it to myself for many years. That was another successful point that I came to in the process of curing my depression.

I also made it a point to take not only my priorities seriously, but also other peoples priorities serious, attempting to reduce occurrence of priorities not accomplished correctly for the proper goals materialized. I figured I should attempt to look for other peoples potential mistakes as I was told that the inattention to being correct and precise was inferior business skill and not time and cost effectual. I didn't let any negative feelings come into play when looking for mistakes in my co-workers productivity; I didn't base my criticisms of someone's product on emotionalism or let race, religion, sex, or what seemed to be irrational conclusions made by my co-worker to factor in my decision as to how to amend the flaws I saw in a product and correct those flaws in an empirical, objective manner for constructive business. I also wanted to instill in my co-workers a sense of semi dependability, in pursuit of what I call proper business attitude where if I take the time to do a job correct, then perhaps my co-employees would also do the same, and try to do things right for an ideal, productive work environment. You can say you work 'hard', but how can you prove your work and the studies you engaged in for your occupation were some kind of hardship in all peoples mind? Or in any peoples mind? What I would be looking for is empiricism in assessment of a project accomplished, and an attitude that work isn't a burden but something to take serious as people depend on you to be rational and turn out the best product possible, like a product I would care to patronize myself because of the highly desirable quality of the product.

Another step in my attempt to beat depression is that I need to realize that I am going to die eventually and there is nothing I can do about it. We might live to 85 years, or our life may be made shorter by some disease or accident. Know that there is plaque in our heart tissues that we wont be able to stop from building up until it stops our hearts. The soul is said to be eternal, and whenever we leave this Earth, our life isn't over. Believe me, the actual process of giving up the ghost isn't painful; I've had out of body experiences before and I was engulfed in great feelings of peace while catalepsy. God's judgment will determine how we will live the rest of our life after our life is continued off of this Earth.

I made it a point to pay attention to how I am physically comfortable most all of my waking hours. The United States government has made it so that I have plenty of food and shelter, and I am so comfortable I can't see how anyone can be against the U.S. government for any reason. If I lost my income, there are usually agencies that make it so I don't starve, and have a clean place to sleep at night. Therefore, how can I or anyone be resentful of the way our government looks out for us? When things don't go my way, I can be thankful that I live in America. In Myanmar, the Philippines, and many Asian countries, as well as Africa and Central/ South America, people don't have government food/shelter assistance and many of them come to the U.S. and Europe just to eat and have a roof over their heads, as well as make it so they can get adequate medical care. As righteous as the U.S.A. is, how do I or anyone really have anything to be resentful of while living in America? If you read this statement and don't live as nice as I live in America, those families that are richer as or more than $2000.00 a week didn't always have that kind of money. They worked for it, and you may have to work for that type of life yourself if that's the life you seek. I don't really place value on idols of people to have to be resentful of bank accounts of people, or their material possessions. How can you or I resent happiness of people? Usually you get to eat, and sleep at night. Comfort is mostly all I know, so I don't have to be in resentment that I didn't get all that I wanted. 65% to 70% of the world gets what they need for sustenance and shelter. Most people that read this are surely falling within that 65% to 70% category. As good as mere existence is, I took that into consideration before I let myself get depressed about a life that doesn't really seem to be anything of hardship. Remember, you were not born knowing the concept of hardship, so why let others make hardship a reality? Hard is all in our mind. I made it a point not to enter into tasks with the attitude that the task is going to be difficult. How do you know a task will be difficult? If you do have problems with life, consider that life is only temporary and you don't have to worry over things that are trivial compared to the Judgment.

I made it a point to look at how I was depending on love and sex for my happiness, and observed that I was not really involved with anyone who cared enough about me to want to see me succeed as much as I care. Does your sex partner care to see you succeed in what you call success, or are they just using you for money and sex? The society I live glorifies sex and I find that I can save time and money by masturbating instead of involving myself with people who don't even have my best interests in mind just so I can say I have a sex partner. I noticed that my orgasms from masturbating are just about as good as the orgasms I get from the sex act. Yes I like women, but why become involved with people sexually to the point it becomes a financial shortcoming? Why would you be pride less enough to let sex dictate how you behave? Do you gain more intellectual prowess by sucking up to people for sex? Unless you want money, drugs, or love, I don't see gain of anything more than orgasms that you can get from masturbating by believing that you absolutely have to have sex acts with people. I didn't have sex until I was brainwashed at 17 by Hustler and Playboy into thinking that I was missing out on something I obviously didn't need to engage in before I made a success at school and work. I deprogrammed myself out of sex with people for no other reason than to fit in and/or have orgasms by using empiricism. With empiricism I feel so much self-esteem that I don't even need drugs or sex to feel as good as I felt when I used to use LSD in my teens. Empirical outlook is so rewarding that I got pride from being of rational mind constantly, and made it so I don't suffer at all.

It came to the point where all my drug use didn't give me pride, or the intelligence to live pride. So I made it a point to start the process of ridding myself of drug habits. I noticed I was happy, very happy, before I started to use illegal drugs. What could keep me from being happy if I gave up illegal drugs? The San Francisco Drug Court Program told me I was depleting some chemicals that are naturally occurring in human brain tissue every time I did certain illegal drugs. These naturally occurring brain chemicals(endorphins) give feelings of well-being in brains not intoxicated with illegal drugs. I learned that when I did amphetamine and marijuana, I was causing my brain to quit making a brain chemical called dopamine. When I did cocaine and alcohol, I was causing my brain to quit making other chemicals(endorphins). If you abuse illegal drugs, your brain becomes physically dependant on those illegal drugs to replace the endorphin brain chemicals you don't produce anymore because of illegal drugs. That is what doctors say makes people addicted to illegal drugs. I took it upon myself to see if I could make it so I was happy without illegal drugs, like before I started using them. It was a matter of pride, and I wasn't going to let some drug dealer dictate to me when I am to feel pleasure. I did what the drug program told me to do and questioned values of people and places that cater to drug use. I started to notice I had more money for things I wanted from not blowing it all on drugs. When I quit using illegal drugs, I noticed I could enjoy my food more. A fruit juice or an occasional Clif bar became more delicious when I beat illegal drugs. I found I didn't even need to take all of the pain killers that the dentist gave me after my dental procedure thanks to not being poisoned by illegal drug addiction. In essence, I made it so I could enjoy life all over again, like I was reborn. I had physical withdrawals at first, but I was rewarded with being sober enough to make rational decisions again, like before I was an addict. I even enrolled in college classes on becoming sober. I did B grades when I attended school again, instead of flunking most of my classes like when I was a drunk. I believe that the pride I got from regaining my sobriety took me beyond a state of depression that I had fallen into. I would be surprised if I ever went back to illegal drug use again. Like I said earlier, my accomplishments from my sobriety have given me pride so wonderful that I don't want to be a puppet of illegal drugs that didn't enhance my intelligence or make me anything that I call success.

A point I considered when trying to beat depression is that I was always told a good friend can get you through times of trial. I don't believe you should guaranteed trust people to get you through any trials you may encounter at life. A lot of times people you think are your friends don't want you for any friend. Many times my supposed friends, including some of my family, dumped me as soon as they saw the party was over. Life of going clean and sober requires that you reject illegal drug use, and that may mean you have to do without friends for an indefinite amount of time, perhaps years. As soon as I realized that, I wasn't lonely for friends and found comfort in sobriety without need for friends to comfort me. My sobriety is more important than friends and family.

One more point I took notice of was that I should never let myself get depressed by being caught up in someone else's anger or depression. Like I wrote earlier, I can feel empathy for people, but not sympathy. When I was in nursing school I was told that the proper attitude for medical professionals is not to become emotional over the patients you care for as emotionalism of any kind, outside of a warm and friendly manner when going about patient care, is considered the antithesis of focusing on your medical priorities in a totally objective manner. As I agree with my nursing school instructor, I don't let sympathizing with emotions of anger and grief blind me to my priorities, as that isn't the scientific approach I'm to use when administering patient care. That ideal of objective, rational manner of thought carries over into how I deal with emotions of anger/anguish in people. I can't let fear/hate in people interfere with my judgment. If people aren't empirical enough to see that emotions outside of happiness aren't rational, aren't even natural as far as I'm concerned, then I've got to keep a clear mind and help those that are angry to see life in a more rational light. I now feel that if people who are angry fail to understand why they don't have to be angry, and that anger is irrational and obsolete, then I need to be sober and empirically rational so as to let them see that if I can be calm, then maybe they can be also. If you can't predict life, and life has no guarantees that things will always be cheerful, we must realize that it's up to us to make life better. And you may have value to someone who sees you happy. Try to show kindness and see someone's life happier. My reward for helping people is the pleasure I get from just trying to enrich someone's life experience with positive, optimist views that I feel can bring harmony between people. That personal agenda makes me glad instead of depressed at life. And I'm not preoccupied with obsolete anger that used to stifle my ability to reason. Then I'm not blind to reality enough to be pissed off anymore. This is the end of my lesson on how I cured myself of depression. My steps for depression free living have served me well for the past 25 years. The peace of mind I get is like justice served; justice that you may want to see if you be of an egalitarian character. Some people have said there was no such thing as justice. I want to tell you now what I think are some of the constituents of true justice . . . justice for peace of mind for us, and for all the Earth . . . for lasting mental utopia. Please continue to read . . .

Chapter 9

JUSTICE

The definition of justice is to do righteousness and fair play to others. But all peoples idea of what's the practical thing to do to isn't always agreed on. All people aren't Christians, and some are heathens. If you chose to practice the concept of being vigilante, then you might think that whoever makes the rules and has the power to enforce those rules makes for what is the right behavior to live.

I think justice is realized when society has not turned people into cynics, and people can still think in a rational manner and not relegate themselves into stereotyping people. For people to judge people by reason of their ability to perform tasks that maintain the upkeep of their society and what they do to attempt to make their society evolve in levels of education and technology seems more like a citizen who has some value to peaceful human intercourse as a whole, as does most citizens who willingly participate in social reform efforts. Justice to me is when you can look at people that serve society as friends instead of making racism criteria as to who makes for the proper friend, sex, or business partner. Justice is when society can rise above stigmatizing those who will not conform to racism, war, flags, and religion, and live in peace with those in dissent against orthodoxy some see no reason to have to obey. Justice is the day people are so proud they don't need to take vengeance against those who slandered them. Justice is served when you can want to see all races of people succeed in what they as individuals call success, as long as that success isn't degenerate to upkeep of an empirical civilization.

Justice is when non Christians can still be Samaritan because they were not heartbroken irrational cynics. Justice says the lie of schizophrenia is degenerate sophism and inertia from the pseudo scientist. Justice is to not fall for conventionalisms without question. Justice is when those that perpetuate the lie of schizophrenia are exposed as no more than obsolete, as schizophrenia cannot even be measured by scientific calibration devices, and it cannot be proven that hallucinations even exist. Justice is when you are empirical and rational enough that you don't ever have to be lonely, afraid, hateful, or jealous because of anyone anymore for the rest of your life. That is what type of consciousness I'd like to see in all of the human race on this Earth; that is thought which I call true justice. I don't suffer anymore over other peoples ways different than mine. Empiricism made me want to be a leader, and one who cares to see the whole Earth succeed in mental preponderance over dogmas that seem only to serve inertia instead of making all people leaders in rational thought.

I believe our Earth's governmental process, while moderately successful, can stand for some improvement. I'm now going to present my ideas for an overhaul of the United States government, a reform I believe is of empirical measure. I will also attempt to show how a one world government can be implemented and successful as well. While there's no guarantee that war will ever be eliminated on this Earth, I believe empirical manner of thought will show mankind how to think in a way that diminishes the need for war, as well as mental anguish among Earth's citizens . . . let the Earth's people evolve in intellect for a safer, more bountiful world for us and our posterity . . . for mental utopia. Please read the following statements . . .

Chapter 10

A GOVERNMENT FOR THE WORLD

Here is how I think the United States government and many of Earth's governments could stand some reform, for an attempt at mental utopia for human kind. First, if American high school students are struggling to compete in math/ science with Asian and European high school students, then the U.S.A. should try to eliminate history, psychology, literature, and sociology, and replace them with math in high school/college/university campuses. You don't get math/science skills from Richard Wright, Mark Twain, Flannery O'Conner, O. Henry, or history books, or the sophism of sociology and psychology as so called empirical science. History, psychology, literature, and sociology, like art and music classes, don't instill in students powers of critical thinking, and are the type of classes schools should consider obsolete to the point of eliminating them altogether. The aforementioned literature authors only perpetuate racist attitudes that are contradictory to empirical thought and upkeep of social harmony and Western civilization. All Earth's schools should specialize more in electronics and math.

Republicans say to reduce U.S. debt, the U.S. must get the U.S. credit rating down so government can loan you and small business money. Who's going to loan money to people that aren't of technical education or enough business income to afford to pay money back? Considering the size of the U.S. population, and with 238,000 plus college/university graduates not able to find work as of 2011, how does anyone know that there are enough jobs to be had in the U.S? Loaning money doesn't guarantee keep businesses afloat. Republican Newt Gingrich called President Obama the 'food stamps president', but how will anyone prove that there will be enough jobs in America or the world in the next 50 years? Republicans can't make small business hire more people, and neither can democrats. There is no guarantee republicans will make more jobs for America. In a San Francisco Chronicle newspaper of 1994 there was a front page article that stated there will be mass hunger from food shortages in the U.S. and abroad by year A.D. 2100 because of overpopulation on the Earth. The less people on the Earth, the more jobs and food per individual. We may be seeing some of the effects of overpopulation right now considering the unemployment situation in America. Just what do republicans and democrats think they're going to do about that, short of measures like the Chinese government does when they put a limit on how many children a married couple can have? It seems like republican tax payers are not into more taxes so they and their children can have a chance to afford college and make odds better for them to have food and shelter in times of dwindling job prospects and rapidly evolving technology. U.S. television news says if governments print more money inflation will occur. I believe that usually inflation occurs if there's oil and food shortages. Money was printed by the U.S. government in 1998 when government introduced new 5, 10, 20, and 50 dollar bills. There are new currency of quarters with one of the 50 states of the United States of America on them that have been printed within the time period of 2001-2008. Inflation didn't occur after U.S. paper money printing in 1998 for 10 years until 2008, when oil prices went up. If it's too expensive for the U.S. government budget to print more money, then why doesn't the president do what is necessary and borrow enough money from our friends in Bahrain, Oman, and Saudi Arabia, so as to print enough money to pay them back and pay China as well, for reducing our national debt and giving more money for math training programs here in America? That's also a way to fund Medicare/ SSA payments for our retirees, and military budgets. There's seemingly no food shortage in the U.S.A., and there possibly won't be until 75 years from now, so I don't see what's treason about printing more money. The U.S. Bureau of Labor Statistics said automation and artificial intelligence outsourcing may also inhibit job growth, with job growth in those areas at about 7.3 million job openings from now to 2018. Every job that can be automated could possibly be turned over to robots. Unemployment may rise more than 10% and students may opt for trade jobs that might not be automated, like nursing or machine/robot repair jobs. Massive unemployment from a automated world of robots will make any U.S. president appear to be the welfare/food card president, including any republican president. For students, they may want to consider getting the highest math training possible.

What seems traitorous to some Americans is the constant funding of Pakistan by our U.S. government. Every year for 15 years republicans and democrats gave Pakistan $5 billion dollars a year in funds to fight terrorists. Instead of America continuing to fund Pakistan, why doesn't the world's governments help Pakistan's government starve terrorists, and crush the terrorist insurgence in Pakistan once and for all? Why doesn't Pakistan ask the whole Earth's military for that kind of assistance if they are the friends of the United States and the Earth and deserve any alliance the U.S. gives them, or any help period? The citizens of the United States could use some of those tax dollars our government sends to Pakistan every year for Medicare, highway and transportation improvements, math schools for the United States, etc. How can republican tax payers and republican congress members cry about democrats spending too much tax payer money and then let republican and democrat congress members continue to abuse American tax payers and fund Pakistan $5 billion dollars every year, especially when it is said that certain members of Pakistan government are in cahoots with several terrorist groups that are enemies of the United States? It doesn't seem like Pakistan is an ally of the United States or any country, and needs to be cut off of funding from the U.S. and all countries. That seems like useful reformism. Back in 2006, news journalist Walter E. Williams said in a news column editorial that the United States has an arsenal of 18 Ohio class submarines, and each one is loaded with 24 Trident nuclear missiles. Each Trident missile has eight nuclear warheads capable of being independently targeted. Mr. Williams says that means the U.S. alone has the capacity to wipe out states that support terrorism. He also goes on to say that the loss of life through conventional weapons used in World War 2 far exceeded loss of life from dropping of atomic bombs on Hiroshima and Nagasaki. Vigilante means no one is holy or evil, and you can't prove all anti war pundits are race mixers, and not genocidal abortionists (murderers).

U.S. soldiers and most all U.S. military have gone to serve in the military on a volunteer basis. Neither they or their families felt that it was 'evil' for any military service member to possibly become a casualty, or kill people.

I read a magazine article where it said the current movement to cut carbon emissions does very little and at a very high cost. Cutting carbon emissions is also politically complicated since it requires every nation on Earth to agree to reduction goals. If the Earth spends $800 billion over the next 85 years on the Vice-President Al Gore solution of cutting global carbon emissions, we wouldn't see temperature reductions of more than 0.3 degrees by the end of this century says some of the world's top climate scientists. Global warming will put 3% more of the Earth's population at risk of catching malaria. It does look better for the Earth to switch to all electric cars eventually. A study by researchers from Princeton University says that Ethanol fuel for transportation may double the greenhouse effect of global warming, and that world wide land use for corn for Ethanol would mean corn based Ethanol would not decrease global warming by 20% but increase it by 93% from plowing up land to plant corn which would release carbon stored up in grasslands. Wheat is better than corn for humans. Nuclear energy reactors can reduce global warming. The cost of these nuclear reactors is a big issue. That should tell the president of the U.S.A. to try to get Bahrain, Oman, and Saudi Arabia to loan the U.S. money to print more currency, so the U.S. can construct nuclear reactors in secret, before the E.U.A. finds out, before the E.U.A. can jack up the price of fuel even more until it stifles U.S. nuclear plant building processes. The removal of nuclear waste shouldn't be a problem if the waste material is sent out to radioactive outer space through efforts similar to NASA spacecraft missions. That should be the only reason to send spacecraft out into space, as the gravity and atmosphere of most other planets prohibit human life from inhabiting them. On most all other planets, you will be subjected to being poisoned from the atmosphere or crushed to death from the gravitational pull, or both. Life on manned space trips will perish before reaching planet Keplar B22 unless more powerful space transit exists. Nuclear chemists say the U.S. needs 3000 more nuclear reactors. Scientists also say agriculture trends that allow too much animal manure and crop fertilizer to contaminate freshwater and coastal ecosystems is blamed for eutrophication, which is the depletion of oxygen to support fish, and crustaceans/marine life. And as the Arctic melts, lack of sea ice will yield colder, snowier winters in Europe, Eastern Asia, and Eastern North America. Environmentalists may be looking at genetically modified crops as a carbon reduction technology. Some republicans keep saying there's no proof of global warming, but every major news report and science magazine tells of massive deterioration of both polar ice shelves. Obviously some republicans don't live long enough to have to starve or drown to death from global warming and don't give a crap about future posterity's lives. Scientists are already working on showing how increasing temperatures will affect future weather patterns in the Earth. These scientists hope that their research will help architects design structures that are better suited for the hotter climates of the 2050's and beyond. Temperatures of 104 degrees Fahrenheit will be common in the 2040's all over Europe and the United States during the summer, with warmer winters as well. Environmental restoration projects may create millions of jobs around the world. So called 'green' products are flooding the marketplace, but is this type of product going to benefit the environment? Many personal care products that are labeled organic and safe for the environment are actually composed mostly of synthetics and petrochemicals, and only contain small amounts of organic ingredients. Some companies have consumers paying more for 'value-added' products that aren't much different from the original conventional formulations. If you don't see the USDA National Organic Program seal on a personal care product, then you cannot trust any organic claims made by a given brand until you research that brand. Less meat and dairy products consumption could decrease greenhouse gases by as much as 80% by 2055. Methane and nitrous oxide can be reduced if less meat and dairy are produced and consumed. These gases are produced by livestock waste and synthetic fertilizers; most of that as a result of raising animals or producing the feed used to raise them. Both methane and nitrous oxide trap heat and radiation in the air much more effectively than carbon dioxide. I suggest eating meat and dairy only once a day, 3 times a week, and then fruit, vegetables, and oatmeal for all your other meals.

Medicines that treat illness on the genetic level have come into being thanks to research by European scientists. This medicine works by gene therapy, or transfer of new genetic information into the nucleus of damaged or diseased cells to reprogram the cell, thus repairing it. Ways to do this type of gene repair are to induce viral gene transfer, where DNA is injected into a cell by a virus, or retroviral and nonviral methods. Viral gene transfer is the most effectual way to transfer DNA into a cell, but the body's immune system fights infections, so the chances of the body rejecting the virus are high. Synthetic agents are less effective in getting new DNA into cells but more likely to be accepted by the body's immune system. Scientist are hopeful that gene therapy will be successful at treating cancer, AIDS, and cardiovascular disease, even though it hasn't shown permanent cures. Genetic engineering is a good idea in my opinion. So far, genetically modified grain feed is made to withstand disease and yield more grain also. Stem cell experiments have shown repairs to degenerate human tissues.

Asian countries can put genetically enhanced grain to good use. Asian countries are said to be the most populated, and they will need to make it so there's enough fresh food for their people. A increasing labor force has turned China into the world's top manufacturer. Top priority for China is to learn how to control environmental hazards in their manufacturing process. An effect of the boom in manufacturing in China, as well as other Asian countries, is that the process of catching up with America in technology is now replaced by Asian countries looking for new breakthroughs to maintain dominance in manufacturing. Asian countries are finding it more and more expensive to impose government regulations on manufacturing for proper environmental controls, which makes for slack in health standards in the industrial aspects of some of Asia's businesses. Yet, Asian countries can't do without more economic growth, for a growing population, and for staying a major competitor with the U.S.A. in manufacturing. Many of Asia's population have gotten used to a higher standard of living. More of Asia's people are demanding better lifestyles; better pensions, better health care, and more welfare from their government. That means global food production will need to increase by more than 50% in the next 20 years. Production of wheat and oats should be a primary concern of many nations. Wheat and oats have much more nutrition than corn and rice. A lot of Asian and Central/South American and African countries depend on corn and rice and need a more nutritious diet. To have enough food for the Earth, there's got to be more energy made with nuclear power, not only for less polar meltdown, but for more land to develop enough food to sustain life on this planet. Tearing up land for oil is going to help exaggerate polar meltdown. Electricity by nuclear means should be the concern of the entire planet Earth, including Persian/Arabic oil producing countries. That is a major reform that would give more peace of mind to today's Earth population, as well as promote extension of life for our human race species.

I have some more reforms which I think are not only good for the United States government, but may also be good for the whole Earth as well. I'm going to tell you about my vision of what I call a more comfortable life for us on Earth, starting with some reforms I thought of for here in the U.S., and then branch out to the rest of the world's governments. Some people talk about how they need to find a utopia away from what they consider irrational on this Earth. The previous chapters of this book tell of ways I found to promote rational thought in people. I believe there are other aspects of society besides what I have written about in Mental Utopia that are in need of change. Here for you now are my ideas for more improvements in the governments of this Earth. My ideas for government reform for the U.S and the rest of the planet I call 'my utopia'.

First, there must be a serious effort made to eliminate the tobacco industry altogether. Why does any government tolerate the continued use of tobacco in the face of global warming and possible meltdown of the polar ice caps? That looks like a contradiction in attempts at empiricism. And all the disease that is said to come from smoking (lung cancer, skin cancer, esophageal cancer, heart disease), is not only taking it's toll on human flesh, but sanctioning tobacco use is also contributing to soaring increases in cost of medical care. The government says they want to save money, but then they allow tobacco use, which drives up medical care costs. Legalizing marijuana is also contradictory to decreasing cost of medical care, as pot smokers populations are high in pancreas and stomach cancer casualties. Pot has just as much carbon emission as tobacco. I would hope the federal government of the U.S. and the world would put the safety of the entire human race before the wants of some hedonism minded people who don't care about the health and welfare of anyone, including themselves. If you think you can't give up pot and tobacco for any reason, you live a precarious life. I quit pot and tobacco use after indulging in it for 28 years. I didn't need nicotine patches, but I did benefit from mental techniques for instilling pride like what I described in previous chapters of this text project.

Medications that are called anti psychotic medication should be eliminated, as they are not conducive of any restorative medicinal value and are sometimes too costly for some mental patients to afford, and prescription discount plans don't always offer affordable choices. Seroquel, Abilify, and Zyprexa aren't for hypertension patients, and are contributors to heart disease, and are causes of arrhythmias and obesity. If you don't abuse your Stelazine or Navane anti- psychotic pills because you have a real medicinal need for relief from insomnia, and you've been taking sedative acting medication more than 10 years, then why would you abuse barbiturates? Overdose for suicide can be had from medication that is labeled anti-psychotic medication. But I'm not aware of people taking anti-psychotics for suicide. People taking anti-psychotics should be put on barbiturates, or a sedative with no side effects that cater to heart disease process. If government thinks people are on Social Security disability just to have a drug party, then testing mental patients for anti psychotic meds use is something that I would suggest as a way to weed out abusers of the Social Security system and thus save tax payers and government some money. Pills should be made for the recreational drug users that are depressed enough to want to be intoxicated that don't cause heart disease by the Earth's governments. Cannabis derivatives for 'happy' pills will be good for the ecology and are less likely to be addictive or contribute to heart disease and cancer, and less likely to make stupors that are dangerous to the public or oneself. Government could easily make it so those government sanction 'happy' pills are not for sale to people on mental disability.

Abortion should be a legal right in the United States and everywhere on Earth. Abortion doesn't harm anyone, and to be honest, what would God punish the unborn fetus for? If anything, the soul of the unborn will go to Jesus, and never had a chance to transgress against Jesus, until the time Jesus tells that soul face to face to obey or be cast into the Lake of Fire. At that time would the soul of the unborn decide whether to be saved by Jesus. It isn't up to anti abortionists whether an unborn soul goes to the Lake of Fire or Jesus. Prove the unborn souls of humans go to the Lake of Fire if they aren't allowed to be born on this Earth. No one has proven that yet, not to my knowledge. My only proof that I have a soul isn't known to be evident to everyone, when not one human can prove I gave up the ghost and saw an afterlife like I said and believe I saw. We can see the effects of a society where drug use is allowed, but can we prove calamity for unborn souls subjected to abortion? The recipient of an abortion and the medical practitioner who performs abortions will be judged by Jesus. That judgment isn't up to the republican party, no matter how they swear abortion is the wrong thing for society of America and the Earth. Why does it seem like the majority of republicans are segregationists who don't race mix or preach or take up for that kind of Torah and Christianity if they are so in with God Jehovah and Jesus Christ for their anti abortion stances to be so important? Anti race mixers commit abortion every time they want to put a stop to mixed race births, or choose to stay with their own kind for whatever the reason. No to race mixing is a form of genocide, which is murder.

I do support the death penalty given by penal institutes for all of the Earth. And it's a lie that anyone that supports the death penalty is a Christian. Many republicans are saying they are for pro life and down with abortion in America, then they turn around and also claim they are for the death penalty. Jesus Christ says no one is to be killed and sent to him. The book of Luke says that Jesus sticks with the Ten Commandments and tells humans that thou shall not kill humans. You can't be down with abortion(murder) and be up with the death penalty(murder) at the same time without looking like a contradictory fool. Any politician who is anti abortion and pro death penalty at the same time is a hypocrite and not empirically sound minded to be in office or to seem like they have proper judgment skills to be running your life or anybody else's life with any sort of power of rational thought; not a true effectual leader in objective, empirical thought for me to be voting for them. What about you? I do not have to lie and say I'm a Christian just to get somebody to cooperate with my wants. I don't have to lie and say I'm a Christian so I can get a paycheck. The proof that reducing crimes of murder by imposing the death penalty on murder convicts isn't shown by having a death penalty clause in any government. What you can say is a benefit about the death penalty for any government is that it may reduce the tax payers burden to have to keep someone convicted of murder alive, someone who has proven they are treacherous enough to murder a human, and it is a possible risk to their society for them to escape incarceration. If some republicans continue to say there's no melting of polar ice caps when the news and scientists are saying that polar ice caps are melting, then republicans again are not seemingly pro life or Christian in their quest for dominance in the area of manufacturing.

With a loan from our friends in Bahrain, Oman, and Saudi Arabia, the U.S. can afford to print enough money to pay the loan back and have cash for a reform I thought of that I call a federal training program. My program is for people between the ages of 18 to 55 years old. The training period is for 18 to 24 months for $18.00 an hour or more depending on specific skills learned. This training would be designed to include felony drug convicts who can't use FAFSA grants, because nobody needs these convicts sitting on dole instead of trained and ready for work. My program also calls for methadone administered at the work place, so as to reduce sick leave. My program would make it so you can be trained twice in your lifetime for employment skills, and job placement once you are trained. The majority of type of job skills to learn in my program would be for skills in nursing practice, machine/robot repair, manufacturing and electrician/ electronics training. I believe money for war budgets can also fund the creation of my program. The republicans didn't have any trouble using tax dollars for war movements, so why not defense spending budgets directed at a federal training program? What is the purpose of nuclear warheads if they aren't going to be used as an option to funding conventional wars that eat up tax payers dollars and subject U.S. military to unwanted and unnecessary casualties? The sooner my idea for government reform is implemented, the sooner America will have a population where there's an increased number of technically educated people, and more capacity for manufacturing with far less unemployment.

In considering that all people aren't going to guaranteed conform to or benefit from a federal training program for jobs, another thought I had for government reform is for governments to establish more penitentiaries in each state. Each new penitentiary should be super size, that is, hold up to 200,000 to 300,000 inmates. The money to fund these super size penitentiaries can come from the defense budget, since the U.S. government has a nuclear arsenal that can defeat any army of soldiers that engage in conventional warfare. Why do tax payers complacently go along with politicians who say there's no money for job programs, or the government can't afford to pay for ways of making jobs for those already trained for employment when they do have the money, and are continuing to use your tax dollars for things that are not conducive of attempting employment for the masses, or not ensuring the proper health care/police state for the masses? Do you have to keep putting the same useless type of politicians in office with the delusion that republican or democrat ideologies are empirical choices for so called leaders to be continuing to get paychecks when neither political party in America is making any sort of proof that they can make enough jobs for America and the Earth? Empiricism means you do what is practical, not what a political parties ideology tells you to do, not what your father or grandfather or great-grandfather told you was the right thing to do, not what your race or religion told you was the right thing to do when you see and know it's not the practical thing to do for you and those you care for.

If no country has the will to attempt to induce global harmony, then let this next idea of mine begin it's life in the United States . . . another attempt to reform education and jobs production, and reduce war on this Earth would be to gerrymander countries, starting with the U.S. making Canada and Mexico part of the United States; all 3 countries become one country. Let this process evolve until all of the North American continent and the South American continent are considered one nation. Then try to continue the process overseas, until the whole Earth is one nation. Arabic countries are already revolting against their leaders in pursuit of a democratic style of nation for themselves. A one world currency could be introduced, which would be a plastic card that could be electronically monitored and activated by Earth Incorporated, the one world government. If Earth Incorporated can monitor the currency card, then they can deactivate the card to try to control and arrest those card holders with felony warrants, and card holders who Earth Incorporated suspects of being enemies of Earth Incorporated. All governments who refused to cooperate with the Earth Incorporated government would be taking their chances. The object is to get all the Earth's existing governments to cooperate on becoming Earth Incorporated one world government so as to pool technologies and ideas on proper educational goals in an attempt to make it so as many of the world's people flourish as possible, as well as an attempt to reduce wars on the Earth. That is some of my idea for a possible government reform of not only the U.S.A., but also the Earth.

I say yes to gold, diamonds, and silver continued as legal currency. The electronically monitored one world currency card for all countries participating in the Earth Incorporated form of government would be more durable than paper currency, which would save money, and possibly cost less than paper money to produce. That type of plastic card one world currency might also help reduce carbon buildup in the Earth's atmosphere by governments not having to cut down as many trees.

Since there is no Earth Incorporated one world government in existence, people who travel internationally will still have to get visas. The U.S. should cut visa card use down to only 4 years of stay in the U.S. If the owner of a visa cards cannot produce U.S. citizenship for themselves in 4 years time, they should be banned from returning to the U.S. for up to seven years time before being allowed to return to the U.S.A. If Mexicans aren't legal citizens of Earth Incorporated or the U.S., then they shouldn't be allowed in the U.S. any longer than the time a visa card gives them. Black Africans, White Europeans, Pakis, Hindis, Persian/Arabic, Canadians, and Orientals who are foreigners have to have visas/passports to travel to the U.S., so why let Mexicans stay in America without proper documents? Just what grounds does the U.S. have for giving non citizen Mexicans permission to stay in the U.S. if they don't have visas? I was told by a White man in San Francisco that when he went to Mexico on vacation, he saw all kinds of signs in Spanish language that said for the citizens of Mexico not to rent apartments to Negro race people. So, who really wants or needs to go out of their way for people from a country that tolerates that type of race bigotry? I don't believe all Mexicans are racist against Negroes, but I don't really see what the U.S. is giving special treatment to Mexicans for. No to Mexicans living in America without proper legal documents that every other foreigner has to have. All foreigners should leave the U.S. when their visas expire with no exceptions.

Here's some more reform for you . . . television programs in America and the Earth are proliferate in shows that promote gun violence and murdering people. Why can't the TV industry promote more shows that instruct people in science/medicinal skills when many U.S. schools are behind in math/chemistry, and jails/penitentiaries are full to capacity? There's something congress should be concerned about. If congress and the president of the United States are so Christian and concerned about the welfare and safety of the citizens of this country, then why not more time spent on educational TV to promote science shows on television and in the film industry? Bloodshed and occultist movies make money, but shouldn't TV violence be kept minimal by governments when attempting to produce engineers and presidents out of kids instead of gangsters? I don't see enough movies that show race mixing and people of interracial birth. If I were a politician, I would go out of my way to preach race mixing, along with much more attempt at empiricism for my society's upkeep, and I'd seek TV that didn't overly indulge in redundant violence oriented materials constantly. I believe television programs should be made with more emphasis on harmony between people, not murder, rape, and racist segregation being tolerated constantly in almost all of TV entertainment. Many times, books and magazines are as full of hate and bloodshed as what's on TV. Crime stories have their aficionados, but what about the making of egalitarians in our world? How about more TV with shows preaching love, and more precaution taken to lessen crime on TV?

I hope you will consider my suggestions on government reform as useful, and something to inform members of congress about. It's time for the Earth's governments to change for what I call the better, and stop the lie that politicians are actually doing the best thing for your life and children's lives.

There are people in this world that say they have love in their minds, but racist strife still keeps families and individuals from experiencing other cultures and races different from their own. You can't expect wars to end when people refuse to tolerate different religions and races. My parents taught me to tolerate religions and races different than my own. It wasn't enough. I had to race mix, because how do you know something isn't any good until you try it? I never had to hate other races, and I learned that from experimenting on my own. I found out something that lots of people even in these times just can't see, or won't admit to. I found out that love is more important than race. Let me show you what happened when I took it upon myself to mingle and sex with all of the Earth's different human races. Maybe you can come to give more love to mankind from what I'm going to show you. Read this next passage . . . for love, and mental utopia.

Chapter 11

LOVE IS MORE IMPORTANT THAN RACE

I am a race mixer. I race mix because I feel no shame or regret in race mixing. I never feel that race mixing is inappropriate or irrational. I see physical beauty and intelligence of empirical nature in some of all races of this Earth. I have had some kind of friendship or sex act with all of the different subspecies(races) of the human race on purpose. I didn't have any empirical, rational excuse not to. I don't know anybody who has sex with all races and doesn't discriminate against a particular race. There may be prostitutes who are racially indiscriminate about their sex partners. But I don't know of any people who are educated at colleges/universities, the so called 'upper crust' of any human society who practices and enjoys races mixing with every and any race.

I am a Negro race blood who is fair complexioned(high yellow) and I was raised by caramel colored Negro race families, some of who race mix with White race people. I went to elementary school in a predominately Negro neighborhood until my mother remarried, and then we moved to a mostly White neighborhood. I never really bothered to kiss up to the Negro races I was involved with and stay with my own kind. I always welcomed different race kids into my scene, and the Negro races I hung out with didn't bother to mingle with too many White kids. A lot of Negro friends of mine were paranoid of White kids because the Whites were exceptionally racist in our part of the country(Ohio). My Negro friends would call these redneck Whites hillbillies. I found that the Negroes were just as hateful of race mixers as the Whites in the county where I lived when I started having sex with a White girl. I wasn't interested in only Negro cultures, and the illiterate Negro and White races I grew up with couldn't understand it. I always had a talent for making race bigots look irrational, and I believe that to put down someone for friends or sex because of race is absurd. When will Negroes calling White people hillbillies prove that Negroes are more inclined to empirical method of thought if Negroes listen to jazz and classical music than if they listen to White race rock and roll music? When do Negroes in America imitate Negroes in the jungles of Africa for Negroes not to be just as so called hillbilly as the White race they imitate many ways of thinking from? A lot of Negroes that do race mix are hateful of other Negroes, including other Negroes that race mix with White scenes. I've seen Negroes who are race mixers actually roll their eyes at me or look at me with hatred when they and I are together and around White people, like these ridiculous uncle toms are the only Negroes qualified to be seen as socially acceptable to White races. You may not believe it, but once some White skinheads that told me they don't race mix gave me beer and weed, and didn't even care that I was a Negro race. I didn't hate the skinheads for being comfortable with staying with their own kind, because obviously they were happy and their social and sexual preferences were, although dumb, not my business. Negroes are presumptuous if they think that White people owe them friends/sex, and some get angry that a White didn't want to give them sex. Some of these uncles take it out on me and other Negroes, like immature jokes. I've had Negroes who were Caucasian in lips, nostrils, teeth, and head hair, and were high yellow skinned like Persians and Chinese actually argue with me and tell me they were members of the White race, and that I should kiss their ass because they were White. A girl I used to associate with has a green birthmark on her foot, of a pure blood Irish White race. Green birthmarks of the Irish, plus an Irish with that type of birthmark also having milk white skin instead of having yellow skin is a true White. There are Whites with one blue eye and one brown eye, another mark that only comes in White people. I feel that if you are born out of a sex act where one of your parents was Negro race, then you have Negro genes and chromosomes, and are a Negro race no matter how Caucasian you look. When do Whites call people with a Negro parent a White race human?

A lot of Negroes were wearing prep clothes in Ohio, like that makes them or anyone the equivalent of an aristocrat, or empirically successful at critical thinking skills and chemistry/physics. The Negroes that were patronizing prep styles were usually Negro snubbing types that couldn't even associate with Negroes that were light skinned, or Negroes that were successful at mingling with White people, or any Negro, and you could see it hurt them to see a Negro appear intellectually competent to make a White race look ridiculous in so called logic, and to find Negroes that are not embarrassed by having the nose, lips, teeth, and head hair of Negro races.

You might wonder how I associate with Negroes when the majority of them stay with their own kind. I realize some Negroes just don't trust other races for friends or sex, and there's many Negro hating uncle toms out to gain special status with Whites. Many times I've done girls that were university students in fields of education or science degrees. You may find a psychologist among Negroes that will race mix or make friends with races different than themselves. I try to find race mixer Negroes that aren't paranoid that I sex with White girls, especially if they sex with Whites. It's usually not likely that a Negro that race mixes with Orientals is as paranoid to have a Negro that race mixes with Orientals around his Asian lover as it is for you to see a Negro hesitant to mingle with Negroes that lay White races when their lover is White. Some folks are so hot for White people that when they see a Negro that lays White girls they are racist, and want the righteous Christian minded Negro race mixer that doesn't have anything against Negro males sexing with White females to fail at life. I know stupid uncle toms that have told White women that I was gay just so they could attempt to keep me away from sex with White women. I was fired from a minimum wage telephone solicitation job at the request of some ludicrous uncle tom who wasn't brainy enough to pull White women except for prostitutes. A Hindi race that worked with the uncle told me why I was fired. The uncle tom was so hurt to see that I was more than a GED educated and didn't kiss some White racists ass and put down Negroes that he had me fired, and refused to speak to me when I saw him again. If you're a Negro and race mix with White men or women, or whatever, try to stay with people that are more educated than condescending bigots that snob treatment Negro race mixers, and if the racism against a Negro race mixer is coming from so called white collar professionals(chemists, medical doctors, psychologists), ask them how are they supposed to merit respect from empirical society, or prove with a rational statement that their racism is legitimate. Before you go off and race mix with whatever race different than you, try loving people because they are objective minded empiricists, not because they are a certain race. How does a white collar professional claim to be of rational thought when they are sick to their stomach of race mixers and Negroes, or think of themselves as someone who's word carries any clout in circles of science empiricism thought or leadership position in any society?

Usually, Whites are more willing to race mix with Negroes that show some interest in Whites. A lot of Whites I call pride less told me to lick uncle tom. As a Negro race mixer, I would suggest to other Negro race mixers to question those Whites that say lick uncle thoroughly to see if they treat you as an equal to their White race in giving you Negroes respect that they easily give their own race. Who is dumb enough to trust someone with their valuables in a marriage and beg complement from some White that's not even pride or empiricist enough to treat them with respect except for some pride less jerk, who, if they do lick uncle, shouldn't be looked at by leaders of any government as someone to trust to raise children to be leaders, instead of mediocrity and inertia. Who ever heard of some Negro that was a known uncle tom to be more than obscurity? Just because 90% of Western civilization is of a White man's blueprint doesn't mean Negroes have to deify the White race, like they are dumber than animals.

Negro girls I have had sex with were always paranoid that I would leave them for White race females when they found out I was an all races race mixer. As an empiricist race mixer, I wouldn't leave a Negro woman for a different race unless the different race than my Negro lover was proving herself to be empirically superior intellectually to my Negro girlfriend, not because the other girl was Asian or White. Try looking for empiricist lovers, not just base your choice of lovers only on race. I suggest that to all humans.

I have also had friendship and sex with Native American girls. When I was in the military I met a military member female who was a Navaho Indian. She was from California, and I immediately fell for her because she was so intriguing and physically beautiful to look at. When we went out for dinner, my Navaho friend was so sexually attractive I wanted to sex with her. After dinner, my Navaho friend and I went to a hotel room out on the highway and we had wonderful sex. As I lay with her, I told her how beautiful her skin was. She was caramel colored, with raven black straight head hair shoulder length. I told her she was so beautiful that at that time I wanted to be her skin and hair color. I am yellow skinned, and much lighter skinned than her. I told her my mother has her skin and hair color. The Navaho girl said that she would rather be my skin color, of a Chinese. We had sex all night, then in the morning we went back to the military post. Later I found out that my Navaho friend was having sex with blue eyed blonds and chocolate skin color Negroes also. I had told her in the bed that I was also part Native American myself, a Cherokee Indian like my mom's dad, but I don't know of my Navaho friend ever laying with a pure blood Oriental Asian race. I always thought that the Native American was mixed with Oriental Asian races from thousands of years ago. When I hear about Native Americans, it's always that they don't work for White people. I hear that Native Americans are usually on welfare or SSI, and lots of them don't get past high school. A lot of Native Americans told me they didn't like the White mans government, and are seemingly still sore minded about the U.S. government killing so many of their people to make the United States. Some of the Native Americans reject the U.S. government flag and put it down as inferior to give it respect. Much of the Native American people are into White races, and many of them I talked to didn't like Negroes very much. But even though I am Negro race, the Native Americans I did talk to were very well mannered. Lots of Native Americans tend to be of Latino race makeup also.

I would consider a Native American woman good enough for a wife, as long as she was educated enough of a woman who wasn't worshipping Whites as her superior. A lot of Negro and Native American women seem to think that White skin and race is automatically the right type of people to look at as intellectually superior to themselves. There's no guarantee that anything White is empirically the better educated race. And to be pride less enough to think that a White race is better looking than you Negro and Native American males and females is looking like the media has picked nothing but White races to call beautiful, and you might have been brainwashed by it. I have seen Mexican Indian women and Negro females that were mind blowing in looks, but the White media and many in White society go out of their way to glorify mostly White females, and don't look at Negro race and Native American women for role models as to what's said to be beautiful. Honestly, I have seen greater numbers of Mexican/Native American women who were more beautiful than most all of the White race all over California. Many Negroes that race mix don't take up for Native American women except for some Negroes in California where there's lots of Latinos and Native Americans. There are a lot of

Negroes who only look at White women, possibly from being brainwashed in their youth by White racism. Many times in the Southwest, you'll find Native Americans are quite racist, and will be offended if a Negro male licks up on a White only Native American female, like the Negro male couldn't be good looking or intelligent enough because he wasn't all the way Caucasian. But then the Negro male that's empirical minded may want to seek out races different than Native Americans, because many times these Native American girls that are racists against love making to Negro males half the time aren't even any more than into laying with men that aren't working on property purchases for girls. Many times in the West Native American girls are indeed drug addicts(I've seen such a thing myself), and any college educated Negro male that's pride minded will pick a life partner that's got more on their mind than lying to themselves that a drug user is the only husband that's good enough. Prove White race bourgeoisie doesn't marry Negroes. Can Native Indians prove their people to be leaders more than Negroes?

Hindi girls that I have been with were charmed that I like them. Hindi girls in California are usually looking at men making more as $3,000.00 a week. I believe most Hindi girls are looking for men with more money as $3,000.00 a week, and usually don't mind what race you are as long as you have the proper income. Many Hindis stay with their own kind, but I believe they will race mix with Negroes quicker than Native American girls will, except for Latino race Indians. I've had Hindi girls frown up at me for looking at them, perhaps because I am Negro race. I don't really see Hindi girls as having the powers of redemption for me to care much if they don't like Negroes, unless they have some influence on my income. Most all my life I always thought Hindi girls were finer looking as the prettiest mulatto or Latino or White girl. I like Hindi people, and lots of times they don't have to be druggies, which I can respect. Hindis are usually good in math and engineering, which is something I have never put much effort into in my high school and college years and wish that I had. My cousin had been having sex with a Hindi girl in the past. This Hindi gave me tongue kisses when she saw me, but she always liked my cousin better than me, so she always refused me fornication. We might have stayed friends, but when she broke up with my cousin, she didn't bother to associate too much anymore. Eventually she and her family moved overseas to Asian countries, and I lost track of her. She was really cute. I got head from a Hindi race once, but I never did get Hindi pussy. That's something I would really like to investigate. I would suggest Americanized Hindi girls for a wife for any race of men, as they are usually successful in business, engineering, and medical degrees, and at life in general. Lots of Hindis are not into drug abuse, and usually they know how to make $3000.00 a week pay checks. Go for Hindi races if you're into making it better than just middle class.

White people that I have been around were mostly racist enough that they didn't race mix, but found Negroes to be acceptable as friendships. The Whites I was hanging around with were just like the Negroes that I met in transient hotels in California; they didn't want you for friends, they just wanted you to use you for drugs. Once I got off drugs, I decided to make it a point to try to find girls to lay with that can pull men with university education and a paycheck of $1000.00 a week income. It seems like the more educated a White person is, the more likely they are to race mix. As a Negro that will sex with White girls, I don't go for Whites that aren't into more educated types of guys, like college educated. Most White girls that had me for sex were capable of making $1000.00 a week income, and didn't give me the snob treatment at all.

One thing I noticed was that brown skinned and high yellow Greek gentile White people didn't usually care for friendship or sex with Negroes. Some brown skinned gentile Greek whites seemed so snot nose against sex or friendship with Negroes that they appeared to be physically repulsed by Negroes, and many refuse talking to Negroes or giving them eye contact. I thought that type of snot treatment was highly irrational. I would sex with a beautiful White race brown skinned gentile Greek female, but they are usually anti Negro, and many of them only want blue eyed blond White men for a husband. Even White race Greek gentiles that are high yellow skinned seem hesitant to become friendly or sexual with Negroes. A White race female that is blue eyed and/or natural blond is more likely to give sex to Negroes than brown skinned or high yellow gentile Greek White people. Brown skin Greek White gentile girls in Rhode Island might go out of their way to marry Negro males, but usually dark skinned ones.

White females tongue kiss my Negro mouth but some of their parents are opposed to race mixers in their family, so all they could do was tongue kiss and be friends. That's fine with me, but I don't associate with White people that tell me to stay with my own kind; that is anathema. White girls that said I couldn't come to their apartment unless I had some type of house when the people they have sex with don't have houses and are White race tells me to stay away from that type of White people, because that situation sounds like a racist snob treatment of Negroes. I am not desperate and pride less enough to suck ass like a 5 year old, and treating me like one will only receive rejection as a reward.

I've heard of White males and females who only like the most darkest skinned Negro they can get for sex, and I have been refused sex and marriages from White females because they wanted a Negro that was dark black skinned for their sex and family member instead of high yellow Negroes. Milk white skinned White females that wanted me, a high yellow skinned Negro, were usually a Greek German gentile type, which is usually the main type of White race female that goes for a Negro race for sex. Irish German non Greek gentiles usually pass on a Negro race for sex partners.

Lots of White people don't want another Jimi Hendrix in the universe. Many times Whites don't appreciate Negroes playing guitar in a rock style either. Whites may also be very hateful of original guitars from Negroes. Negroes may lose friends and sex and become ostracized if they try to be original in music. It almost seems like most society only has a 9th grade education, maybe even Hollywood. That's another reason for the what I call educated Negro race mixers to seek out either university educated people who may be more equipped to like Negroes that aren't stereotypes, or seek people who are Christian minded or younger than 30 years old for race mixing scenes. Lots of White races don't want Negroes to play anything more original than a cheap Hendrix imitation. If you're a Negro race trying to play primordial rock and/or avant garde rock, some will call you Jimi Hendrix even when they know you don't play blues or preach drug addictions and heartbreak songs like the mediocre popular music industry, including cornball Jimi Hendrix blues/grief/drugs lyrics of a relic minded pride less loser mentality. It's so hard for some White people to take it that I, a Negro, try to play guitars quasi original and not imitate Slayer 'Reign in Blood', a speed metal genre music that preaches sheep minded Satan worshipping and that isn't proven to be more avant garde than noise records and Teenage Jesus group music, that some Whites get angry that a Negro guitarist lives that doesn't imitate worshipping Slayer music. Some Whites have said Slayer 'Reign in Blood' makes all Negro music obsolete. I try not to play stereotyped guitars. I preach for pride in my lyrics, not mediocrity of Satan worship and blues/tragedy. I seek iconoclasm in my music, even if my guitars resort to some conventions of rock music for intrigue. I really want music that's not based on race.

Slayer music is usually original, but more conventional than what I would call avant garde.

Jazz and classical music might not always preach blues/tragedy, but that's no guarantee the listener of such will be able to deduce life in an empirical style.

Industrial styles of rock music seems to attract White people that don't mingle with Negroes and Orientals. A lot of industrial music is fashioned after the 60s' and sometimes blues guitars. I don't see anything avant garde about the majority of industrial except for Sonic Youth. A lot of Whites that are into industrial don't sex with Negroes and the scene is usually a racist one. I guess some White bigots just don't stand to have to affiliate themselves with Negroes. And they don't need to. Any Negro race mixer should be prepared to get the snob treatment from the industrial crowd at a bar scene that plays those styles.

I don't see why Whites and Negroes that race mix are either for the Negro race scenes or only the White scene. Most pop music is racism oriented, catering to perpetual segregation of races of man against each other. Lots of Americans are racists that have some kind of race bigotry against some race different than their own, or against their own race as turncoats. It takes a chump to wallow in racism all their life, like they had no rational brain power or pride than a hurt animal, hurt because some other race got some idol/icon away from them and their race. I laugh at those that boo hoo race mixers, like they were really, truly going to be cheated by those that race mix, or cheated if they participate in race mixing themselves.

I believe that White women who don't like it to see a Negro that doesn't give them a lick up or complement, or put on like White females are always finer than non White females are just like pride less irrational wimps. I've heard White women tell me they were jealous of me because I was high yellow and said they thought I looked finer than them and wished that I was gay. I've heard dark skinned Negro uncle toms say the same thing.

Why is it that words said to be derogatory of Negro lips, nose, and skin color are offensive to Negroes in the mind of some White people or uncle toms? Anyone Negro that fails to enjoy life and succeed at work because of words of kindergarten minded racist crap from a fool is obviously in need of self esteem, and dumb looking as a 10 year old child trying to look sexual to adults. People that are persistently calling names in race bigotry are seen by me as no more than an asswipe crying their eyes out. If you hurt from being made fun of or from being called some name that people are seriously into laughing at, then you are in need of self esteem, and a 10th grade education as well. Even if peoples criticisms of you lead to you seeing the behavior that you are criticized for as flawed to yourself and others, and if you let other peoples hate or revelations that you aren't empirical embarrass you, then I think you need to remedial back to the 10th grade all over again. Why would anyone's put down of Negro races, or any race, cause anger or embarrassment? Does the person putting you down have the powers to redeem your soul, or escape the Lake of Fire? Do they have the powers to be sexual to you, or interesting intellectually to you, for you to see them as anything more than insignificant? That you were picked as a scapegoat for some chump says the chump doesn't think too much of their own self, except to consider themselves a failure in life.

Many White women have what it takes to get me to lick up, but I don't kiss uncle tom. Most of White women that gave me sex never told me to kiss uncle tom to them. They were in the bed with me as quick as if I was a White man. I noticed most of the White women that told me to kiss uncle tom were high school dropouts, or GED recipients and SSI check receivers, who were only giving sex to other high school dropouts, or some known race bigot.

I noticed that White women who were lesbians were always seemingly snot nose against Negroes, including female Negroes, and if White lesbians prostitute with a man, it's usually with a White race only. Only once have I had sex with a bisexual White female.

Many White homosexual males are race mixers, including with Negro men. I've seen more race mixing out of White male homosexuals than all the so called punk rock liberals who preach down with racism, including female punk rockers. I don't even know of punk rockers that race mix, except in San Francisco. Like industrial scenes, the punk of America usually doesn't race mix, especially in Cincinnati, Ohio. Punk rockers aren't usually seen by the bourgeoisie as worth peoples time anyway, so I believe Negroes would do well to stick with an objectivist type. And if I find a girl with job skills, I don't look at psychologist degreed people. I do make exception for film makers and theatre types as potential friends and sex partners.

I always liked Jewish White people, and White race Jewish females for sex partners. It always seemed like every White girl I was kissing with or friends with was Jewish. A lot of these White Jewish females couldn't sex with me because one or both of their parents didn't like Negroes having sex acts with their daughters, and don't want their daughters to marry Negroes. It's a common occurrence in Cincinnati, Ohio to find White Jewish females being told by their parents not to sex with or marry Negroes. In most all of the rest of the United States, White Jewish females don't have any problem having sex, friends, or marriage with Negroes, except for maybe San Diego, California. I'm Negro, and I've had sex with White Jewish females, but they were from Los Angeles and Las Vegas, not Cincinnati, Ohio. The White race Jewish females in Cincinnati, Ohio that turned me down for sex were mostly high school dropouts, or GED recipients and drug users on dole. These 9th grade dropout White Jew females were also telling me to kiss uncle tom, like they were embarrassed that all they could get to sympathize with their racist cliques was some dunce that would give racist trash prestige and that bourgeoisie would leave behind for society's sake and let go to drug dealers or the food card office, and they didn't even try work or $15.00 an hour employment skills school and chose prostituting themselves, or drug dealing. I've had Ohio born White Jew female chemists who would give me a tongue kiss, but since they were of racists they could only give sex acts to White race Jews and gentiles who didn't even want them for marriages, or didn't have bachelor degrees. Ohio, Indiana, and Kentucky White Jew females are usually racist and don't call too many Negro race males sexual or intelligent enough for sex partners. I've seen White Jew females in Cincinnati, Ohio go out of their way to avoid eye contact with Negro males they attend to at their cash register job at the shopping mall. I've had White Jew males from Cincinnati, Ohio tell me they didn't want to play guitars with Negro race people for musical group memberships. Maybe a Jew living in Cincinnati, Ohio that's younger than 30 years old will friendship and business partner with Negro people. I don't know, and I don't care. I don't deal with Jews from Cincinnati, Ohio who snob Negroes. I sometimes try to avoid Cincinnati, Ohio Jews since they don't usually race mix. White Jew from Cincinnati, Ohio that makes more than $2,500.00 a week type of degree or certificate from post high school institutions will treat a Negro with respect, but I don't know about marriages. Los Angeles Chicago, New York, and Las Vegas White Jews are more into sex with Negroes, in case any Negroes reading this statement are interested in White Jew marriages. Brown skinned White Jew people, especially the female version, are usually mostly racist against Negro races for sex acts. Brown skinned White Jews might tongue kiss my Negro mouth, but many lay White high school dropouts instead of Negroes that have more as $25.00 an hour job skills like myself, just so they don't have to lay with a Negro race I'm told. Brown skinned White race Jews may like to pick blonde gentile White race people for sex instead of Negroes, and some are visibly and verbally racist when a Negro is seen by them to be a race mixer with White races, be it Jews or gentiles.

Jew worshipping was vogue with many high school dropouts I used to frequent back when I was a drug addict, and really popular in Cincinnati, Ohio. If a Cincinnati, Ohio White race Jew is thinking I'm supposed to worship White Jews instead of making empirical decisions as to who and what to give prestige to, then they are as dumb looking as Gomer Pyle in Mayberry. Lots of Negroes who are known uncle toms from Cincinnati, Ohio are also into the practice of being angry if I didn't give White Jews that are no more than grade school dropouts or racist at Negroes more prestige than a gentile, or a non White that's a chemist, engineer, or medical doctor. Some uncles in Cincinnati, Ohio are also angry if an uncle that worships White Jews isn't licked ass to by Negroes. I've heard of White Jews from Ohio, Tennessee, Kentucky, and Indiana that were medical doctors accused of saying Negroes and other non Whites, and White gentiles are to lick uncle to White Jews, or that Jew will reject them for family. Jew worship in Ohio, Kentucky, Indiana, and Tennessee, and all down South, by high school dropouts/GED recipients or white collar professionals preaching it, is anti empirical compared to giving prestige to those that excel in math, chemistry, and engineering, and/or show qualities of egalitarianism, even if they can't be Christian. You might want to give egalitarians preferential treatment. I really don't give special treatment to people just because of their race; that doesn't seem rational thought. And all White Jews aren't in a position to give you a $5000.00 a week paycheck for 35 years for most of them to be thought of as something to worship, as if society outside of Cincinnati, Ohio doesn't have any more brains than a donkey. I am a Negro that will and has lain with White Jew females, and I didn't have to suck ass to them for the pussy. Only Cincinnati, Ohio White Jews were rejecting me for sex. White Jew women I ball are usually 95% from outside of Cincinnati, Ohio, and live outside of Ohio, West Virginia, Kentucky, Indiana, and Tennessee. Lots of gentile White Irish people marry White Jews, and in Cincinnati, Ohio,

Irish White gentiles overtly kiss ass to White Jew people, usually the Jews that are known by the scene to be racist. White Irish gentiles and White Jews in Cincinnati, Ohio are many times segregationist against marriage with Negroes. Usually, half of Ku Klux Klan and skinheads in Ohio are comprised of White Jews and White Irish gentiles. The Alabama White Knights of the Ku Klux Klan say on their web pages that the synagogue of the White Hebrew race has a statement in Jewish Talmud alphabet that says Negro races are nothing but half ape and half donkey species. Looking at all the White Jewish girls that sex, marry, and have children with Negro men in Florida, Michigan, Delaware, Maryland, and the cities of Chicago, Seattle, Portland, and Las Vegas, it doesn't look like all White Jew females are brainwashed out of Negro male marriages just because of some 3000 year old Jew person wanting their race to remain pure of Negro blood. However, many Southern and Midwestern U.S. White Jew people are very adamant about not letting their sons and daughters sex and marriage with Negro race species. The Nation of Islam, a Negro run organization, says that the families of Goldfarb and Goldstein are White race Jews that are the true enemies of the Negro race. I don't know how true that is, but I don't have any anger about White Jews that are anti Negro/non Whites and anti gentile White races. If all Jewish haters of non Jews/non Whites keep the peace, then usually I'm not preoccupied with White Jew racism. If I meet a kind acting White Jewish female, I will hit up on her if she's sexually attractive. But I don't know anything other than friendliness from most White Jewish males and females. White Jew males are sometimes eager to be friends with Negroes, even in Cincinnati, Ohio. It's just not that likely a Ohio Jew female will do anything sexual with Negro men . . . maybe a White Jew female in Chicago, New York, or Seattle perhaps. Most of the time I can tell if a White person is Jewish race blood. I've had Jewish White females tell me they were not Jews, and I could see that they were. Then they would come to me years later and admit that they really are Jewish. Some White Jew girls were proud to be Jews, and told me so. I don't see why a White Jew person would be reluctant to admit they were Jewish. I don't hate White Jews, and I'm sure I won't be hating anyone or anything thanks to empiricism style of thought. My mother's dad is mixed with White Jewish race blood, and I really don't get angry if White Jews ever show hostility towards Negroes. White Jews don't owe any other race different than their race friends, sex, or marriage. I hope White Jews will be open to all races for friends, sex, and marriage, like I am.

The Aborigine race isn't too prevalent in my part of the United States. I used to associate with Aborigine boys in my neighborhood when I was 15 years old, when the kids in the neighborhood would get together for basketball games. These Aborigine boys were very friendly to all races of people in our community, and they were never racist mouthed. I also met a 23 year old Aborigine girl when I was about 26 years old. She was very friendly, and used to hug a lot, and give tongue kisses. She would race mix with her sex acts, but not with Negroes that had high school diplomas. The only Negro this Aborigine girl would sex with was a Negro that was racist against Negroes, a high school dropout, and would steal money and food off Negroes even if they were friends with him. The Aborigine girl's decision that the Negro that rips off other Negroes for White racists to applaud it is cool is because she claimed Negroes need to be shit on because they were Negroes period. She also said a Negro wasn't any good if a Negro didn't kiss uncle tom to White races. I heard this female Aborigine wasn't a high school graduate, and racism is typical of high school dropouts I've been acquainted with. The then 23 year old Aborigine wasn't laying with White races said to be handsome, or more than $6.00 an hour, like she had no more ambition than a 12 year old. She was so naïve she would say White people were more intelligent and better looking than Negroes, but she would sex with the uncle tom Negro hater Negro, as if she wasn't of rational thought, and liked to live contradictions. The last I heard of this Aborigine girl, she hadn't made a GED and was over 30 years old. I couldn't know how someone that doesn't look like any competition to Negroes for the rest of society could be so easily racist. The last I heard, she was single as of her 33rd birthday.

I've seen some pictures of Aborigine women. They were usually not bad looking to me. I've only seen two Aborigine girls that I called beautiful. One of them was a gold medal winner in the 2001 Olympics. I'd date her for a relationship if I lived in Australia. I believe this Olympic games winner Aborigine girl is a university graduate. Usually, I don't hear of many Aborigine people that race mix with anything except White people. I would settle for an Aborigine girl that was seen by me as good looking, if she was college/university educated. I don't hear very much about Aborigine people attending college or university campuses. I hope they will. Every show I've seen on cable TV about Aborigines tells nothing about Aborigines except how they were not really a major part of Australian White society, and many times all I see of Aborigines in Australia is how they are unemployed, or in the penitentiary. I didn't know people eat kangaroos until I saw Aborigines doing it on TV (they were eating the cooked tails of kangaroos in a ritual that's part of the Aborigine culture).

I would love to see Aborigines better off than the unemployment lifestyle and/or the penitentiary. I would like to see Aborigines sexing with and found to be sexually attractive to all races of humans. It will be up to the Aborigine people to become more a part of main stream bourgeoisie Western type societies. From what I see about Aborigines on TV, it really doesn't look like Aborigines are quick to fit in with White societies, and are content in their own circles.

I have had sex with Persian/Arabic women. I met a wonderful Persian girl in 1988 who was into the speed metal scene popular at the time. She had just returned from living in New York City, and wanted to see some speed metal. She asked me if I knew where the speed metal was in Cincinnati, and I told her. She said she wanted a companion for the evening, and asked me if I would accompany her to see speed metal. I did join her, and she was nice enough to pay my admission to the concert and even bought us beer pitchers. We had a great time from the music, and before the evening was over we were having sex acts with each other. We didn't use condoms, which might be dangerous to some, but we trusted each other. We had pleasurable sex, and this Persian female was remarkably beautiful to look at. Many Persian women are, to me, some of the most beautiful females in the world besides some Greek mulatto and White women, Latino women, and Hindi women.

Many Persian/Arabic people are into Negroes for friends, sex, and marriage. I had a Persian male apartment roommate once, who was really nice to me. I've also seen Persians who don't act like they like people here in America. I think Persians that seem irritated by Americans think that many Americans are void of what Persians deem proper morals, and that Americans need to be snubbed. I find Persian females to be as interested in romance with Negro men as quickly as milk white skinned gentile Greek German White women and Oriental females. A Persian male friend of mine told me that many times a Persian father of female Persian children will tell his daughters not to have sex or marriage with Negro males, but he will also tell any male Persian children he may have that it's acceptable for them to sex with and marry Negro females. I've been frowned at by Persian women and given the snob treatment from them just because I looked at the Persian females and smiled at their beauty. Maybe it was because the women were foreigners and not used to American men showing their interest for a beautiful woman. Maybe it was because I was a Negro race, and they were offended by what they may perceive as an inferior race. I was in San Francisco when these Persian females snubbed me, so maybe they were lesbians, but that's really no reason for them to jeer and frown like a dunce.

I think many Persians believe they are more holy than Jews and Christians, but they might be in for a sobering surprise, according to what I have seen. I didn't think it would be necessary to write what I'm about to write, but I feel it should be written. One day in 1989 I was in a restaurant with a friend. He had a blank expression on his face, and kept looking at his right palm. I asked him what was the matter, and he then showed me his right palm. I believe that day I saw what men might say is the Mark of the Beast. What I looked at was a symbol and a number. My friend went to the restroom to wash the mark off with soap and water, but it didn't come off. Minutes later, the mark wasn't visible, and possibly now on his soul. My friend never talked about what I saw on his hand, and I never bothered to talk about it with him again. I'm keeping his name a secret out of love for him, and also because I don't want him to get the same treatment as Pope Louis of A.D. 1553, who was beat and burned alive at the stake for confessing that he had committed a sacrilege. If any Muslim religion practitioners of Persian/Arabic people, and other races into Muslim ways think Islamic Jihad against non Muslims is legitimate, I say they are wrong. As far as I'm concerned, Muslims are the real infidels when against Christ Jesus. The mark on my friend's hand tells me Jesus is the religion that saves you from eternal punishment. Non Christians will receive the Lake of Fire, even Muslims. If you want to escape the Lake of Fire then you won't do any sin, including murder thru Jihad. If you have the Mark of the Beast, you are obviously so vain gloried that you must be really happy at life, and possibly have a mental utopia many people don't or won't ever receive or comprehend, and may not have any use for this text project. I still feel many people will have use for this text, so I will continue to write.

I've seen a lot of Persian women in California that go for nothing but blue eyed blond White non Persian men, and rarely do I see Persian men and women having romantic looking relationships with Orientals. I don't care for Persian women for marriages if they are Muslim.

Don't go to Persian people with any tattoos, especially tattoos of maskim, which are pictures of demons, unless the Persian is a non religious type. Persians are highly offended by tattoos if they are orthodox Muslims, and may turn against you.

I have heard that maskim(demons) are race mixers. The maskim Nimrod, of the family of Ham, was said to be a race mixer and half goat, half human shaped. Lilith is also heard of by me to be a race mixer. If you are offended by race mixers, you will possibly be sick all your time in the Purgatory, since demons are said to be lustful for humans and will condone race mixing. All the malechim(angels) and maskim(demons) in the afterlife are either Jewish or Persian races I'm told, and are not racist against Negroes or Orientals. I don't believe that angels will be performing sex acts, especially not with humans, but demons might be into sex acts in Hell, including with humans.

The sodomy act is illegal in Persian/Arabic countries, where sodomites get put to death if caught. If you want a person that's a sodomite for a sex partner or marriage, you might not get to perform sodomy with a Persian/Arabic race.

I've read how Persian/Arabic men having contempt for women, especially foreigner non Persian/Arabic types of women, will gang rape women as a way to humiliate them in retaliation for some type of insult to Persian/Arabic men, or just to be machismo. Ex Iraqi leader Saddam Hussein had his military rape their prisoners if they were suspected of being traitors to the rule of Mr. Hussein. The soldiers of the Hussein regime would not only take a man prisoner, but also his wife. The supposed traitors to Saddam Hussein would be subjected to torture even if they were not proven traitors. Under torture by the Hussein regime, a man may have to watch his wife being gang raped repeatedly in the same room he's locked up in. Then after soldiers finish beating and raping the man's wife, the man is beaten for hours, then forced naked and anally cauterized with hot irons until he can't pass bowel contents. Then both prisoners are executed by a firing squad. That was a standard form of torture and execution in Iraq for years if some were of political dissent. I believe the present form of punishment for political prisoners in Persian/Arabic countries these years is imprisonment, and sometimes beatings or hangings. A man or woman that is said to have committed sacrilege in a Persian/Arabic country will possibly be dismembered or decapitated, or simply hanged.

I will support sex and marriage with Persian/Arabic people for myself, other Negroes, and all races of humans on the globe. I believe Persian/Arabic people are highly sensitive to sacrilegious behavior similar to irreverence named by the book of Koran. The Koran is said to condemn types of behavior that are also seen as sacrilege by the King James bible. So, basically a Persian/Arabic Muslim expects Christians to know what is the correct behavior for man to live on Earth. All Persian/Arabic people obviously aren't into Jihad, and many Persian/Arabic people are very Westernized and will not be shy to involve themselves with a nice, friendly person into romance with them, even those that are not Muslim. I don't see myself going to Persian countries for marriages, but a Westernized Persian woman will always be on my agenda for getting myself a lover. I don't really have anymore to comment about Persian/Arabic women, except that I think they have possibly the most beautiful race of women out of all races of women on the Earth. Persian women turn my mind around for a solid wife. I don't know of too many Persian women that are not attractive. I don't marry any Westernized Persian woman I can get, but I feel they're the prettier race.

I have had many friendships with Latino people. I had sex with Mexicans and El Salvadorians who wanted me for a long term sex/marriage partner. Many times I've wanted Latino people for romance, and many were not overly racist against Negroes.

Some El Salvadorians aren't into Negroes for friends or sex. I've been told that Negroes aren't wanted in Honduras, Costa Rico, Nicaragua, El Salvador, Guatemala, and Mexico, and that if Negroes visit Honduras, Nicaragua, El Salvador, and Guatemala, they will be killed.

A lot of times Puerto Rican girls are into sex with Negroes. I've seen many Puerto Rican people, men included, get into romances with Negroes. One thing I noticed about Puerto Rican girls I hung out with was that if they could get a White race non Latino man instead of the Negro they sex with, they might dump the Negro man they were sexing with and start to sex with the White race instead. I've seen the same of Mexican women a lot of times also.

Some Latino women say they are Negro race members, but usually a Latino will say that they are of the White race. I always thought Latinos that were part Indian blood were actually Oriental races, not pure White race, and that Latinos that were not part Indian blood were the only Latinos that were really pure White race.

In San Francisco, it's common for Negroes to get with Latinos for friends and sex partners. Every place else in America, except for some parts of Texas, Illinois, New York, New Jersey, Ohio, and Florida, a Latino usually stays with their own kind instead of Negroes. Latinos are big on White races for friends and sex in many U.S. scenes if they race mix. I believe Latinos identify more with White races than Negroes. Many Negroes just don't go for White culture as easily as Latinos. It's not easy to find Negroes that are into hardcore rock guitar music, or White pop rock, except places like New York or California. Maybe Negroes feel they just aren't going to be accepted as easily as Whites accept their own and Latinos. Like I said, a lot of times a White race that's college educated will sex with Whites that aren't even 9th grade graduates instead of Negroes that are $18.00 an hour or more just so the college educated White doesn't have to sex with Negroes. White race high school dropouts or GED only White races snob Negroes out of sex more often than college educated White races.

When I learned guitars, I was instructed in Spanish classical styles. I always appreciated Latino culture, and found Latinos to be superior in guitar playing to most all guitarists I've heard, except Dominico Scarlatti, Lol Coxhill, Hugh Cornwell of the Stranglers, and Andy Gill of Gang of Four.

If you appreciate Latino culture like I do, then on occasion, try Salvadorian cuisine, which is as savory as Greek/Persian Mediterranean cuisine.

One thing about Latino men. If a Negro man or White man is hanging out with Latino men and they start talking about getting sex with women, a Latino man may go out of his way many times and try to get his Negro or White friend a Latino woman to sex with. I don't really see this done for Negroes by White non Latino men, who usually keep the non Latino White race females all for themselves and their own race.

White European Spaniard girls have been very friendly with me, and have given me a phone number to call them so I could join them in Spain for wine. I heard White girls from Spain were very accepting of Negro boyfriends for sex partners. However, I don't hear of many Italian women from Europe into Negro men for sex. Italians in America usually appreciate Negro men and marry with them frequently. Many times Latin races, Spanish or Italian, are interested in Negro men for lovers all over the world, but more than likely you find that in America. Most all of my female White race lovers were some type of German Italian, or German Spanish, or Jewish German Italian Greek.

Even in America, I've been told, Latinos don't always like non Latinos, whether they be Negro or White, in their neighborhood. I've heard a White guy that was from San Diego tell me when he walked thru a Latino neighborhood in San Diego, he got stabbed in the arm with a pocket knife by a Latino guy. A Negro guy told me that he tried to get a job at the car wash in Los Angeles, but the Latinos that worked there ran him off the job with death threats. I've had Latinos throw beer bottles at me yelling racism against Negroes (I don't know how to spell it, but the Spanish word for nigger sounds like this:'my-yah-tay') when I walked thru the Latino neighborhood in San Francisco. Some places, like Jersey City, New Jersey, I heard there were White power Latinos that physically attack Negroes and are openly opposed to Negro race. In Highland Park, California, a suburb of Los Angeles, Negroes were picked to be snubbed out of the neighborhood by Latinos, and were sometimes killed with guns for having properties or rentals in that community, or just passing thru that community on foot. That was as late as 2005.

One thing about being a race mixer . . . I usually find females of all races that are openly into friends with races different than theirs, but many times they tell me even though they would gladly have sex and marriage with me, their parents are opposed to it. I'm happy that many Latino girls are able to race mix with Negroes, and it is highly desirable, seeing as how beautiful many Latino girls are. It's also good because many Negro girls are racist against anything that's White oriented culture, and Latinos don't usually have a problem with White stuff, like rock music. And the White female usually doesn't race mix as quickly as Latino girls, except for younger than 30 years old White girls, and White girls in Michigan, New York, Connecticut, California, Oregon, and Washington State, or post high school educated White girls.

Usually, a Latino race doesn't expect Negro people to lick uncle tom like the Negro was the equivalent of no more than 5 year olds in a brain contest, or not as of any more value than something you disrespect on purpose and make out to be only second or third class status. If you're a Negro and someone is telling you to lick uncle tom, you may notice it's usually the treatment you get from non Latino White races, like Latinos have more pride, from more education. But, I've actually heard that businesses in San Jose, California that mostly hire or are run by Latino races won't hire a Negro race for work unless the Negro race is legally married to a White race. I don't know if the White race the Negro needs to be married to for gaining employment has to be a Latino, or any type of visibly White race member.

For a 30 year period I was in love with Latino race people. I don't speak fluent Spanish, but Latinos would appreciate it if you will learn Spanish. If a Latino girl finds out that you non Latino guys can speak Spanish, they will be hotter for you, and it will be easier to get them into the bed for sex. You non Latinos shouldn't be presumptuous and think Latino women are all into pot smoke either. I've been with Latino women who were not into pot smoke, and usually they were college/university types that were more likely to be clean and sober, only taking wine seriously. I usually don't turn down a Latino woman who is sexually attractive and is high school/college/university educated, as long as she's not condescending, or a psychologist type. And Negroes shouldn't count on too many lovers from Latinos that are born in Central/South American countries, as they are not as interested in race mixed marriages with Negro people as much as Latinos born in the United States or Puerto Rico. To be honest, usually the more white the skin color of a Latino, the more chances are that they don't sex act or marriage with Negroes. And, yellow skinned Negroes are seen as, but not all the time, more interesting to Latinos for sex/marriages than darker skinned Negroes, except to some Puerto Ricans and Cubans. As a Negro, I don't see myself visiting Central/South America at all.

Out of all the races of people I have race mixed with, Orientals are my favorite race. I will still consider sex and marriage with other races besides Orientals. I love the kindness and intelligence of the Oriental people, and the beautiful looks of Oriental women. A lot of times, American TV doesn't show very many Oriental people. In San Francisco, there are thousands of Oriental women that are unbelievably cute. The Oriental women I've seen in San Francisco were so cute that they were as cute as the Oriental women I've seen on some Korean Airlines TV commercials.

I've seen Orientals of many countries that race mix with both White and Negro races. Many times Negro and White races in the U.S. military go for race mixing with Orientals. I look at Japanese, Chinese, and South Koreans as sexually attractive. Filipino and Thailand women seem to especially favor Negro lovers for sex and marriages. Cambodians, Vietnamese, and Myanmar people have been seen by me with White and Negro lovers. Hawaiians and Samoans mostly prefer their own kind, but some Samoans do like Negro people for sex and marriages. Sometimes a Samoan man will be racist against Negro men marrying Samoan women, but then he won't care if a Samoan man marries a Negro woman. Some Korean men don't like White and Negro race men with Korean women. I heard that some Japanese people that were native born in Japan didn't like too much about the U.S. Chinese are said not to like to have direct eye contact with people, including their own race. A Chinese race may feel it's disrespectful of you to look them in the eyes, or disrespectful of them to make eye contact.

I haven't really had too much sexual contact with Orientals, except when I got head from an Oriental once. But I have had dinner invitations accepted more than once by Oriental females. I really didn't stay with the Oriental girls that accepted my dinner dates because I didn't stay in town long enough for those girls and I to become romantically involved.

I usually prefer an Oriental girl that is yellow skinned, the same color as a Persian race. I also like Oriental girls that are milky white color. There are Oriental girls that are light brown skinned(tan) and also chocolate colored. I'm sure I would go for the brown skinned Oriental girls too. I'm so into the Oriental race face looks and how Orientals are culturally into peace and kindness, that I'm sure I'd be happy no matter what skin color an Oriental is. I like Oriental girls' head hair, their lips and teeth, and usually they are easy to get along with. Rarely have I come across an Oriental who was a cynic, and wanted to see people fail just for being different than an Oriental.

I've heard that the Chinese people think that North and South Americans are undisciplined savages, and a heathen people who are violent for nothing. Many Oriental foreign exchange students at American universities stay with their own kind, and don't mingle with too many non Orientals. I believe these type of Orientals are possibly going to return to the Orient and don't really support associations with Americans, who are possibly thought of as not trustworthy. The country of China has more people practicing Christianity than all of Europe and North/South America combined.

If you ever visit the soup kitchen or the homeless shelter, you may find that you don't see too many Orientals in those establishments. Neither do you ever find too many Hindi races in that situation. At least not in the East coast of the U.S.A. The Oriental people in America are very tight minded; half of San Francisco real estate is owned by Chinese people.

Many a Chinese female is similar to Hindi females, and will be usually prosperous to most men's liking, for men that admire the life or bank account of a white collar professional.

A lot of Chinese that live in Canada are into race mixing with Negro and White races, but a lot of these Canadian Chinese are not into the United States, and some of them wish the United States of America would be destroyed by nuclear warfare, warfare made preferably by China.

A lot of racist White people used to tell me not to sex with and marry Whites. I'm sure I would also marry Chinese, Korean, or Japanese women, whom I feel are really more attractive than many White females, both physically and intellectually. Most Orientals are not only just as pretty as White race females to me, but Chinese are not usually the ones in American society that are preaching race bigotry against Negroes that marry outside of their race. Chinese aren't usually coming up with organizations in America that are racist against Negroes that marry Chinese. You never see that from any type of Oriental race in America. Chinese, and most Oriental races, have so far been seen to be beyond open hostility against Negroes having sex and marriage with their people. This type of calm, rational approach from Orientals concerning Negro marriages to Oriental people does make it seem like those that live in America preaching hate against Negroes that race mix aren't any more than undisciplined savages . . . like dumber than animals.

The Reverend Sun Moon church in South Korea had some people from their organization living in San Francisco, California when I lived there. Reverend Moon died around the year 2000, and he was into preaching the King James bible to the whole Earth. Reverend Moon had branches of his church all over the world. One special thing about Reverend Moon was that he liked to preach race mixing to all people. He would stage mass interracial marriages between White women and Negro men, Oriental women and Negro or White men, and televise the marriages, which were usually done in the country of South Korea. I had the pleasure of visiting Reverend Moon's church affiliates in San Francisco. The members of the church had been living in S.F. for longer than a year when I dropped in to see them. I had read about the meetings Rev. Moon church had in S.F. from a flyer on a utility pole. Anyone was welcome to attend the meetings. The meetings were held in a rented house two times a week. The people that were running the church proceedings in S.F. were mostly Korean and Japanese people, both men and women, who were born overseas and visiting. These people were paid living expenses to stay in California for a certain amount of time and preach bible lessons to the community. After I listened to some bible lesson from Rev. Moon's disciples, everyone in the room was called to dinner. Plenty of delicious Asian food was served to the guests (Asian food is my favorite). The hosts sat and ate with the guests. I was attended to by a lovely Japanese woman named Yoshiko Watanabe, who was very happy that people were interested enough in Jesus to visit the church meeting. She found out I was single, and asked me what kind of wife I was looking for. I told Yoshiko I didn't think I qualified to be a Christian, but I didn't think I was too good to treat Christians with respect. I also said any race of woman would do, as long as the woman aspired to do Samaritan acts, even if she couldn't be a true Christian. I told Yoshiko I especially cared to be in a marriage with an Oriental, because I liked many styles of Oriental cultures. Yoshiko said that when people who join the Moon church marry, the Moon church asks them not to divorce, and to marry for life. Yoshiko also told me her church believes that all races of people should love each other, and that it was good for all people to race mix with all races. It tickled Yoshiko and another female member of the church staff that I said I marry Oriental females. She and her friend thought that was very good, and they thanked me for loving their Oriental people. When Yoshiko told me she had to return to South Korea and her husband to continue to help Rev. Moon preach the Christian gospel, she said I could come to Korea to live permanently with the Moon church, as long as I wanted to dedicate my life to preaching the King James bible and race mixing. I told her thanks, but I didn't want to change my citizenship to that of a Korean citizen. I still remember Yoshiko. She left the U.S. right around that Christmas, and as a token of friendship, she gave me a coffee mug for a holiday present. That to me is further proof that you can find truly respectable people in other places outside of American life. I hope to remember Yoshiko Watanabe all my life. If you are reading this Yoshiko, may Jesus bless you, your husband, and your church for all life. I could certainly use more righteous people like Mrs. Watanabe on this Earth, couldn't you? I'm glad for the Moon church, and I hope it continues to thrive.

For those of you looking for race mixing, there's San Francisco, California, which is said to be the capital of race mixing by the U.S.A. Today newspaper. In San Francisco, I've seen Negroes accompanied by Latino and non Latino White people arm in arm, and some even with mixed breed children in tow. In S.F., I've saw a Hindi man married to a Ethiopian woman, and Negro men kissing Hindi and Persian women. In S.F., I saw an Oriental man walking arm in arm with what looked like his lover, and his partner was a Hindi woman. You may find all types of race mixing in S.F. everywhere you look. One thing about S.F. is that there are a whole lot of homosexuals, so don't be discouraged if you try to race mix in S.F. and don't get anywhere. In S.F. I once hit up on a White woman who was kind to me, but she refused to get involved with me for dinner and sex. I saw the same White woman two weeks later, and she was sitting on the pavement tongue kissing with a Latino female. Seattle, Washington State and Portland, Oregon are good places to find race mixing. I'm glad to have met White people from Seattle who were interested in having Negro roommates come and live with them. The males of that group of White people from Seattle didn't care that the females of that group were hitting up on Negro males for shack ups. I've had several other White females from Washington State hit up on me for a Negro boyfriend. The state of Michigan is a place where many White women prefer Negro males.

Outside the U.S., places like Toronto, Canada have many Oriental women who seek White and Negro men for life companions. Vancouver, Canada also has many race mixing Negro and White females and males for anyone interested. Spain and Germany are always said to be big on race mixers. Thailand girls love White and Negro men in Thailand, but beware of the AIDS virus, which is said to be carried by many Thailand women.

Larry Flint's Hustler magazine does wonderful pictorials that many times show explicit sex acts between race mixers. I support Mr. Flint for showing race mixing in many of his magazines over the years. I would like to see Hustler pictorials of White and Negro men with Hindi girls, and more Oriental women on Negro males also. Maybe Mr. Flint can find some brown skinned White Greek gentile females for nude pictorials, and couple them with White men, and even Negro men as well. I think I've seen brown skinned White Greek gentile females in Hustler having sex with blond White men, but not with Negro men. I've seen brown skinned White Greek gentile females having sex with Negro men in videos from Sin City Videos of Las Vegas, Nevada. I'd like to see more grey eyed raven black haired milk White German Greek females in Hustler magazine, especially with blond White men or Negro men. I want to see brown skinned White Jew women with Negro men for sex in Hustler magazine also.

In the back pages of some sex pictorial magazines there are advertisements for how to get girls for sex. If you send off for some of these sex services you may get something similar to swingers magazines. Many of the girls that advertise themselves for sex acts in these magazines are also race mixers, and they will indicate what kind of race mixing they like, or a lot of times the race of their potential sex partner isn't important. Swingers magazines usually have five or six race mixer White or Negro females per magazine. If you feel like sex with total strangers eager to sex act in race mixing fashion, you might want to purchase a swingers magazine, or some magazine that does nude pictorials.

If any of you readers are race mixers, you may have already checked the internet for race mixing services. There are at least ten different American web sites exclusively for the race mixer. The internet has race mixing clubs that will try to get you the type of race mixing partner you seek. Just be prepared to have employment, and some type of credit card (pre paid credit card or credit card from a bank) and you're all set to find that perfect race mixing partner. Usually, the internet race mixing clubs offer most all races of the Earth. There may be web sites for international race mixing. In America, I found out that there are a lot of Orientals involved in searches for people into race mixing. I don't know of any internet web sites that have Aborigines into interracial dating services.

Many times, your town may have free local weekly news papers that have romance sections where people look for sex or marriage partners. Depending on what part of the country you live, if you look at these free weekly papers you may find some people right in your town that are into interracial dating.

I hope that the Earth, especially the United States and Central/South America, will accept race mixing more often. I preach sex with all races different than yourself for each and every individual on this Earth. I want the Japanese, Persian/Arabic, Hindi, and Jewish races not to be so condescending to Negro people and try to use them for sex partners. I want brown skinned White Greek gentiles outside of Rhode Island to sex with Negroes. I want Aborigines to seek White race society instead of remaining clinging to their Aborigine culture. If White races call themselves seekers of evolution of human species in harmonious and technologically more advanced societies, then why don't Whites, and also Hindis and Negroes, specialize in creating in Negro races a desire to do engineer degrees, instead of saying concepts like psychology, sociology, and literature are valuable for critical thinking skills. Literature as art is based on nothing but racist condescension/presumption from all races that say literature is guaranteed art, and of value to the degree literature is still seen as something that's mandate to a so called proper educational curriculum in American schools. I don't believe courses in critical thinking for problem solving are standard in many Ohio schools, and not found in very many schools in a lot of the East Coast either. Many times American society has not sought what I call justice for all races of humans and has not bothered to instill in American youth the desire to think and live in empirical assessment of our Earth's societies.

If you love someone, either of your own kind, or another race different than your own, I would think you would want to see them happy, and not hung up on racism. If those of you who have children who are kind to all people, no matter what race the people are, I want you to be rational minded and try to accept your children's interest in friends, and even sex, with races different than their own. What do stupid hicks that are the shitpaper of race mixers prove by turning their noses up to race mixed marriages, when there is no biology text that can prove there is something wrong intellectually or physically with race mixing? Race pride seems no more than dumb herd animal collectivism, not pride from being the preponderance from your own accomplishments, since all of your race isn't proven to be creator of the doctrines that cure all disease or cause evolution in technology. And hurt is not pride, for those of you offended to the point of sickened by race mixers. If you hurt because people race mix, then you can't be of rational mind or pride, not anymore rational than the usual 5 year old child. Dumber than animals are desperate to see people stay with their own kind. Will staying with your own race guarantee you success with your own race?

I want race mixing for the whole Earth. I don't need a herd of collectivist animals that can't think or feel good about themselves without the lie that staying with their own kind guarantees them success in business, math, medicine, or art/music. Or pride, something I don't believe many collectivists have too much of. Empirical assessment of the possible inertia in evolutionary process from collectivism needs to be made, for an attempt at propagation of leaders in the world, not angry, irrational fools, like most racists. I will now give you a statement that I feel is the most empirical, rational way of dealing with those that cling to the same way of doing things that their parents, or those they were raised by, have done all their life, without any questioning of why they are so rigid in their beliefs, as if their life will be truly ruined if they didn't remain faithful to conventions they can't prove are necessary for happiness. Are you guaranteed success or failure if things don't go the way of the masses, the herd mentality many were raised with? I feel it's right to question parochialism, especially when parochialism doesn't always seem comfortable to me. I want to be comfortable, and I am when I'm empirical, and of rational thought. Here's my answer to rigid collectivism, and my excuse for you and I to perhaps try a little individualism . . . for an attempt at primordial thought . . . in quest of intellectual evolution of a human species . . . for mental utopia.

Chapter 12

COLLECTIVISM VERSUS INDIVIDUALISM

Collectivism is the theory and practice of attempted ownership of land and the means of production, perhaps as in nationalism. Collectivism can mean a group of several or many people, compared to an individual. Do you believe people are rational when they seek the approval of groups of people that they haven't questioned to see if those they seek approval from are of empirical, rational mind? While there is nothing new in the universe according to chemistry texts, there are blueprints patented that show originality in molecular manipulation of objects. Original patents with only one author are possibly of the mind of an individualist. The idea behind creation of products that are of suitable quality is that the product is suitable for yourself in an ergonomic fashion. Then, as many humans biologically perceive comfort with similar senses perception organs as most all other humans usually experience, the product suitable for yourself may be seen as suitable for others. I believe that type of accomplishment may give a person some pride. I think much pride less ness is from obscurity, and obscurity seems to be no more than mediocrity. We must rise above egoless mediocrity of collective thought done without empirical question so as to foster the intellectualism of an empirical individualist, and instill thought processes for thoughts that are creative enough to transcend not only mental contingencies perhaps brought on by emotionalism thru collectivism, while also teaching children to transcend obscurity, and to transcend beyond the present levels of technology. While there is no guarantee that individualism spawns creativity, do you complacently allow the herd to pick and chose what is right for you? Does conformism to your so called peers blind you to happiness that you seek? I believe pride from empirical, rational productiveness spawns individualism, and the will to excel for your own preservation, and the preservation of your values. Even if your empiricism only amounts to inertia, you may have pride from success at rational thought. Herd mentality collectivism that depends on others approval for self esteem can't really depend on others to get you what you call success. Did your race guarantee your bills paid? Did a White race that makes a paycheck, however they make that paycheck, make that paycheck because they were White race, when Negroes and Orientals are to get the same amount of paycheck the White race made for the same job product that a White race works? Why would people want a particular race not to excel in running of government, or science industry, like the bourgeoisie wants to have to do the work that all races of people have no excuse not to know how to do, for preservation of Western style of civilization? All herd mentality types are not guaranteed to buy into someone's pride less ness for you or anyone to think that the herd can be depended on to get you your success as an individual. Most race mixers I've seen were uncles that only buy into one race's culture different than theirs because of the race of the culture the uncle was sucking up to, not because an individual or collective of the race the uncle was sucking up to was guaranteed out to instill empiricism and pride in every other individual of the Earth, for attempts at reducing wars and promoting rational thought in all humanity. I have questions for the conformist that looks for the familiarity of staying with their own kind to attempt guarantees at success, and looks to be using herd mongering as a pacifier to somehow make everything 'right' . . . Why let styles of clothes or music represent your claim to charisma, prestige, or self esteem, like you're only 12 years old? Why do you think sex or race mixing is somehow provocative, like you are as greenhorn as if you were born in A.D. 1765? Being hurt because people won't give you sex is as laughable as a monkey and ludicrous as 10 year olds trying to look sexual to a 35 year old. Learn to masturbate, or afford to buy prostitutes. Why do you think you need to lay with anyone, like a child might think, for you to have to be gay? If you had true pride, you'd masturbate instead of live as a homosexual, and resentment from failure to maintain heterosexual relationships is no excuse to just give up and be gay. How do you know you can't have success at heterosexuality, or that you'll guaranteed be successful at gay lifestyles? There's no proof any gay marriages will be any easier than hetero lifestyles. And to be gay is the same perfidy as any sodomy act.

Are you thinking that people who try to get you to conform to them when you don't want to are irritating? Emotionalism isn't hard to beat. You were never shown in any chemistry text that you need to act any way you see other people act. Or any way you've ever seen humans act of all the behaviors you've seen from humans all your life. There is no math equation to my knowledge that proves you will experience lack of rational thought if you don't conform to racists, religious types, sexism, materialism, or music genres that may be staple to your race from sheepish collectivism. You weren't told by your teacher at school to be a racist, or a homosexual, or heterosexual, or a druggie for comfort. If you are doubting the credentials of your teacher to instill empirical manner of thought in you or children, school yourself and children in critical assessment of life, and question the things you were told if you don't feel comfortable with your lifestyle, or are irritated by people different than you. There was a book at one of the college campuses I went to that you may be able to buy if you want to attempt to bolster your capacity for rational thought. To see if you can order a post high school text that instructs people in critical thinking, contact Cincinnati State Technical College at www.cincinnatistate.edu, or call 513-569-1500. Now you can see for yourself, if my word isn't good enough, how critical thinking is applied, and how critical thinking lessons just about preclude sociology and psychology as basis for rational thought.

If you're proud to be gay, and I'm offensive to you because I'm proud to be straight, then how are you proud at all? Pride from sex preference, race, flag, and bibles cannot be truth if you're offended into a state of a hurt victim because of other people's differences concerning sex, race, flag, and bibles. I say pride doesn't come from collectivist ideals of racism, sex values, flags, or bibles. I continue to believe much pride comes from an individual receiving prestige in what an individual believes makes them look smarter than others in their society, or the rest of all humanity. Questioning convention (empiricism) makes for objective, rational assessment of life, which gives me pride without any complement needed. If you want to be a leader beyond sophism of race, flag, and bibles, then learn pride from empirical methods.

I believe people cling to herd animal mentality out of fear that they don't have prestige of being distinctive compared to others in or outside of their social circles. Some people fear looking dumber than others in society, possibly because they aren't empirical enough to make valid argument to defend any type of individualism stances. An individual is what asserts itself to take charge, so things might not go wrong for that person when it's time for that person to win, and empiricism can be used to temper ego for rational attainment of pride, as the rational may spawn pride. Then you stand apart from the mediocre, and have value and self esteem from being a distinctive individual. That further justifies the concept of individualism as rational thought.

Fight the sophist war mongers to the death if they attempt to kill you if they cannot think to embrace nihilism. I can stand alone with happiness from empirical, rational thought, and the pride I get from such thought, to the point my existence is more important than those that give a lot of prestige to the temporal. Fight for your life, not for somebody's idols/icons that don't provide nourishment. What does an animal fight for? Do you claim to be more intelligent than animals? You don't have to fight for pride when rational thought makes pride, so there is no prestige for others because of how much money they have. Is it painful that someone can buy more food or baubles than you when they are not guaranteed any more life, or pleasure in life, than you? How does prestige guarantee pride? How does lack of prestige take away from empirical assessment for the rational? Rational promotes practical, which I feel makes pride. When lack of prestige is not able to diminish pride, then that should justify your attempt at individualism, and allow comfort while in an individualist stance.

I believe that not needing prestige from others not only enhances pride, which fosters individualism, but makes it that much easier to look for preponderance, and not stoop to mediocrity that may come from clinging to overt traditionalism. And while living individualism concepts may not guarantee creativity, mediocrity may become less attractive with pride from standing alone to the point you seek to raise your standard of living, while pride also tells you not to let others hold you back in attempts at evolution, especially when there's no guarantee people live to see themselves or anyone evolve. Evolution of a human race species over the level of technology and convenience that most people in Western countries seem to appreciate looks to be an ongoing quest for some individuals. Those that attempt evolution of the human species in technology and convenience are obviously not letting the inertia of those uninterested in rising above collectivism stop their pursuits. Those that have embraced the power of pride and have happiness from individualism are the potential leaders of tomorrow. The power of empirical leaders is influential in fostering attitudes of being rational. Empirical thought is for upkeep, if not growth, of a society. When leaders take it upon themselves to attempt improvement of a society, they are initiating that attempt from the assessment of an individualist. Collectivism breeds inertia and complacency, and is not the catalyst for evolution of a species. Modern is an abstract that can't be measured except for time. What man may say is modern may only be primordial in it's molecular construction, but the chance for the primordial diminishes with the mediocrity of rigid collectivism. I have heard that necessity is the mother of invention. Some people need to transcend mediocrity. We will need individualism to transcend mediocrity. Sticking with the rigid convention of never accepting anything different than the herd in a manner that is almost religious, that is diminishing liberty. Who is opposed to liberty, when liberty is how America got to where it is in the world today? The majority of people that adhere to mores and taboos of American society were given liberty to initiate those mores and taboos centuries ago. What is the law of the land and said to be appropriate conduct is of an individual's assessment that a collective group came to agree upon. The concept of vigilante should tell anyone that individualism is a valid choice of behavior for anyone. It isn't about what's good or evil, but who has the most power that determines what is the law, and what conduct is appropriate. Empiricism should instruct on the rational use of power for your benefit, as well as for the benefit of others.

I'm now going to address instances of overt collectivism that I considered not conducive of evolution of a human species over strife and animosity. My experiences with collectivism were such that much collectivism has begun to be seen by me as of the irrational, and has been relegated to the point of absurd and ludicrous in instances when collectivism does not show itself to be warranted after being examined under the scrutiny of empiricism.

I really had a difficult time adjusting to other children at school when I was in kindergarten. Children, and even the teacher, would pick me for a scapegoat. When several boys would jump me for a fight, I was the one that was going to be punished for it. Girls would come out of the cloak room with wet paper towels on their eyes and tell the teacher that I punched them in the eye, and I hadn't seen them all morning until that time of the alleged incident. I remember one afternoon during reading time, someone yelled out loud that I had said a 'bad word', and soon the whole class was in agreement that I had indeed said something said to be offensive perhaps by some moralist. Of course, I had said nothing, and was sent to stand in the corner the rest of the reading period. Then I was punished for the so called infraction. Why was I being targeted for victimization? This attack on me was done seemingly every week that I went to kindergarten. I believe that I was under persecution because I was the only white skinned child in the classroom. The rest of that kindergarten class was also Negro like me, but they were dark chocolate skin colored. The teacher in that classroom was also dark chocolate skin colored. I believe I was ostracized because it was 1965, and racial strife was plentiful. I believe the parents of those children that were persecuting me were fooled into collectivism of down with White races, including white skinned Negroes, because of the racist climate of the day. I didn't let that mistreatment of me turn me into a down with Negro races act, like I didn't have the rational thought process of more than a animal for brains. Even today, Negroes are still snobbish against me, possibly because of my light skin color. In 2009, I've had a Negro female so called friend of my mom roll her eyes at me after I was introduced to her. This was immediately after I had just shaken her hand. This Negro woman actually turned her lip up at me and sneered at me as if I had done something wrong by merely looking at her with a smile on my face. Yes, the woman is chocolate skinned, and I only dealt her with friendship, since my mom always speaks so well of her. And I'm sure the woman believed I knew she was getting engaged to be married. So what was the sneering and jeering about? Perhaps the Negro didn't like white skinned Negroes, or Negro men period, since the woman was getting married to a White man. I would have told the Negro woman I didn't hate her, but she was so obviously full of blind hate against Negro men I figured she was too disturbed to even bother with, except to tell her to seek therapy. Collectivism ideas of Negroes are inferior to White men is something that makes people look rustic. If you are hurt by Negroes showing you love and glad for you, then you are irrational, and irrationality is not seen as practical when the word empiricism is in the dictionary. I wonder if that Negro woman that couldn't stand me smiling at her with friendship would be angry if she found out I'm glad to see her with a White man, or some other race different than Negro races, and really wished that all people would consider sex with all races. If she lies and says I was trying to come on to her when I'm sure she knew my mom told me she was getting married, well, I've seen better looking and sexier females than her, and how does the woman know I would be interested in her? I noticed that White race women seldom roll their eyes at me at parties, unless it was a White race party guest that I was told beforehand that she was racist. And then, I didn't want to talk to what I was told was a racist for sex. I only approached White racists at parties to see why they had so much hatred for races different than them, and for race mixers. The majority of White females usually want to be friendly, and show interest in a Negro male's business, or want to know if he's successful, or see to it that he does things to be what he considers success. The majority of females I saw rolling their eyes at Negro men were Persian, Hindi, Latino, and Negro females. It sometimes seems like White females were raised to have better social protocol than many non White females. Assuming that Negro males are inferior intellectually is a sophism and not rational. Assuming that White races are always more competent at empirical method of thought is sophist, and irrational(illiterate). Apparently any woman rolling their eyes at Negro men who are obviously not interested in them is under the influence of collective racism against Negro males, something which I believe was started by cuckolds who are not self-esteemed around Negro men who like White women. The person that's hateful of Negro men hasn't proven to all White races that all Negro males aren't intellectually and sexually satisfying to White women, or all White race. Does the woman that rolls her eyes at Negro men for only looking at them prove she's of such an exalted status that she has found the equation that solves war, famine, and disease, or of such intellectual preponderance that worshipping White races makes any and all White race capable of cure for all disease, or medical professionalism, or competent in engineering? Even engineers are not proven guaranteed to always know empiricism method of thought, which includes all races race mixing and tolerance of such. Incompetent empirically is rigid adherence to collectivism.

Even though White girls weren't rolling their eyes at Negro males in my 6th and 7th grade years, lots of them were beginning to get racist. They said they mainly stayed with their own kind because of their parents telling them to. Collectivism of racism against Negro children by White children was proliferate in my early years, and I didn't really care too much, because the Negro girls were usually just as pretty as the White ones to my opinion. As I got older, it seemed racism turned many Negroes against Whites in my part of the country. It also seemed like the White race females were more openly into race mixing than the Negro ones. I still can't figure how people let themselves get so racist that if someone of a Negro race did some act that wasn't seen as socially acceptable and civilized, all the Negro race was somehow responsible for it, like that type of thought is rational, and what men call 'logic'. It seems some Negro uncle toms hate Negroes more than the White race, like they don't have the rational thought process of dogs and cats, and want to be seen as illiterate in their delusion that White always makes 'right'(or empiricism). White race uncles for up with Negroes that I've seen usually don't hatemonger on White races. Could some Negroes be collectivism minded enough to let White racism take their concentration away from empirical, rational thought, like they were inferior as what I've heard White races say of Negroes, that Negroes didn't have rational enough thought to be leaders of Earth's societies, and not fit to raise posterity to empirical thought for leaders made? All the Negro hating uncle toms in the world cannot diminish the power of empirical thought of whatever race of man that implements such type of thought. With the will to question conventionalism in an empirical manner comes the power of rational thought over the absurd.

After my 8th grade season, I was sent to an all boys Catholic school. I was one of only four Negro kids that went there. Every day I went there I can remember some kind of racism against Negroes. I also experienced people who were questioning me as to what was I doing attending Catholic school when I wasn't Catholic. I was even asked that question by several of the teachers that worked there. I don't see what difference it made that I wasn't Catholic and attending a school of so called Christians. If the students and staff there were truly Christians, they should've been glad that I received the word of Jesus, as I'm sure Jesus would have been glad too. The persistent racism I experienced at this Catholic school wasn't anything I would call Christian. I even had a teacher speak racism against Negroes to me in front of other students. I'm not angry about the racism I received at Catholic school, but it is consistent with what I heard about Catholics, that they were largely opposed to Negroes and intermarriage with Negroes. I don't need a human religion to show me how to interpret Jesus. Just read the King James bible. Then you can either buy into it, or reject it. All mans religion preaching on this Earth will not be good enough, as if man can be totally trusted to be a Christian. Jesus will decide who's Christian, not the Catholics.

There is a collectivism that I do praise. It is the collectivism of behavior that people exhibit when they say they are Christian, then go out of their way to make you a member of a Christian organization. People that live according to Christian ways are always trying to make you feel wanted, and it seems that a person who is a true Christian wants to see you saved in Jesus. If that type of person that wants to see you saved isn't saved themselves, at least they are concerned for your soul. That kind of Samaritan and egalitarian that wants to see you saved is a righteous person who I think is a good role model for posterity, compared to so many cynics I run into that are so misanthrope they wish people would fail at life. What good is it that people fail, instead of people empirical to the point of rational, for upkeep of Western style societies? I used to work at a Cincinnati, Ohio YMCA, and I was really impressed at the caliber of people that worked there when I did. They were not hard up for racism, and were not the misanthrope that I see so much of today. The YMCA specializes in lifting the spirits of the community, and emphasizing harmonious co-existence between all of the community it serves. Some branches of YMCA have special day camp programs for children of all races to get to mingle with each other and learn to tolerate those differences, as those differences are very slight considering most people are only human. The day camp teaches kids about nature and the environment also, and that we must work together to preserve nature and humanity as well.

I believe that many people want to fit in so as to feel secure in love. I know of people that go out of their way to be considered original in thought, and fashion. I feel pride wants to be seen as distinct from the mediocre, from the collective herd. Until I was about 17 years old, I wanted to fit in with my age at the high school. Most all the kids of the same race wanted to look like everyone of their own race, or some wanted to wear certain brands of shoes and jeans to be in with the so called 'cool' people, or just any kid of their age. Every guy liked the same thing, the same TV show, the same book. Lots of kids wanted to be different than the grown ups. The thing is, it's still like that for many kids today. Yet I never see any kids that are between 12 to 19 years old seek a life style that begs for the primordial. I believe seeking the primordial helps a kid, and anyone else, attempt to present themselves as leaders, which is more needed by those that might be seen as leaders than mediocrity, which if mediocrity isn't degenerate, it is inertia, which isn't the way a species evolves over the level of Western society in the Earth today. Why do we need to evolve over the level of social intercourse we live today? Because while hatemongering doesn't stifle those that are of empirical mind, hatemongering stifles objectivity in non empirical minds, turning them degenerate against non bias problem solving. The collectivism of empirical manner of thought is one of the few collectivisms that seems immune against the irrational, if you are of a truly objective, empirical mind. Think no convention without question when wondering how is rigid adherence to conventionalism practical. Some have said they want to be free, and want to be original. Can you be anymore than a clone of someone else that came before you? The best way for you to be primordial(original) is for you to try to come up with a better blueprint for upkeep and transition of your society, then the Earth. Beyond aristocracy is the evolutionary that didn't need to be free, because that person was already free of the collectivisms that cater to mediocrity and stifle the plebian not accustomed to objective empiricism way of thought. How can you be secure in love when trying out empiricism on society when so many are closed minded in their racism, sexism, religion, and how they strive to be fashionable, or one better than you with no more than the baubles of the Earth, or status seeking to get prestige from someone no more than obscure in supposed value to leader types, or the bourgeoisie, or less than bourgeoisie? Pride from empiricism is how I live in peace when I see I have no real friends except for some family. Empiricism makes it so I won't need family, because the pleasure I get from the rational manner of empiricism precludes need of feeling loved. While love is a good thing, you may have to live without love if your martyrdom to empiricism is of the nature of true peace and happiness. You should learn to love yourself. You are your best friend when you are not victimizing yourself with degeneracy of clinging to the herd when it doesn't get you to the point where you lose irrational fears. Fear is not objective thought, or rational. If you live in fear of not getting peoples approval you are making a slave of yourself. Cheer for the death of slaves, and the birth of individualism. Individualism is the tool for happiness, and true freedom beyond man's idols.

Some people worship music records like they can't think rational thought, especially teenagers and some high school dropouts. I've seen people throw away their lives arguing over who plays the better guitar statement, like that makes you capable of being socially acceptable to more than the welfare office. When do guitars make it so you have job skills, or capable of empirical thought for proficiency in problem solving? Who plays better guitar is an individual's assessment, unless you're just so conformist that the most corniest, most bent on kissing ass to stereotypes of what a collective race said was guaranteed very talented guitar is how you size up talent. If Wes Montgomery guitar is good to millions of people, and made Wes a millionaire, then how can some racist who said blues and Negroes period aren't talented guitarists prove that Wes wasn't talented compared to grind core guitars? It's obvious that race plays a important role in how music is said to be talented or not. I always tried to appreciate all types/ styles of music, as I didn't want to appear to be no more than crass and dull looking compared to the executive producer of a major record company, like CBS/Sony or Capitol records, who will give a listen to what has intrigue in music effort, and doesn't seem to turn down musicians as employees just because of race or style. It takes a more empirically educated person to be able to appreciate more than one kind of music, like they are not rustics who seem to thrive on racism. Borderless market is what I read in a business law book, and it looks like the executive producer at CBS/Sony and Capitol records has a clear, rational grasp on that concept, compared to so many racists who can't stand Negro music unless it's played White rock style(Jimi Hendrix), or Negroes who don't like White race music, like Cro-Magnons that don't have love for anyone different than Negro races, as if to attempt to punish all Whites for not giving Negro race music and accomplishments as much prestige as White race idols. Trying to push your race down people's throat when you don't have any respect for other races is presumptuous. Rational thought means I didn't need anyone's guitar statement for my excuse for self-esteem and desire for someone to look at me with respect. There are rock groups today that don't even need guitars to sell records, so what does your favorite guitar statement really represent, other than a relic? If you make guitar statements to make money, well, borderless market . . . there's possibly a market for it, so don't be docile if you're a guitarist. I still play guitar, but I also like noise records. Noise is good when done according to my educational tastes. Maybe eventually I'll switch to only trying to put out noise records. Noise isn't as lucrative as a conventional music record, but nothing ventured, nothing gained. Rolling Stone magazine gives their opinion of who's the top 100 guitarists in the world every year, but they don't really prove that all the guitarists they list as the best guitarists in the world are more than icons \ of a drug user, and of the caliber of Andre Segovia, Francis Tarrega, Ibanez, Dominico Scarlatti, Julio Segares, Wes Montgomery, Jeff Hanneman of Slayer, Hugh

Cornwell of the Stranglers, John Ellis of the Vibrators, Al DiMeola, and John Scofield. But who's dumb enough to worship guitars like 12 year olds? I believe electronic music/noise is more futurism than guitars. Just don't expect me to worship electronic noise records, or guitars, or anything period. Well, maybe brown skinned Greek White girls bare feet at least.

I've been confronted with instances of collectivism concerning sexual stereotypes since I was in the 8th grade on. Next, I will list some major stereotypes that I've heard over the years, and I will dispel the hearsay for you.

When I was in the 8th grade, I heard a Negro guy say that White girls were better than Negro girls, that White women were smarter and prettier than Negro girls. Well, having had sex with some of all races of mankind, I can tell you that the Negro females were just as sexually fulfilling as the White females I've laid with. I had one Negro girlfriend that was way more willing and caring to do anything and everything in the bed with me than all White girls I ever had sex with, except for two White girls. As for White girls being supposedly smarter than Negro girls, well, nobody can really prove a White woman is smarter than a Negro woman. All I can think is that one mans god is another mans dog. What's right for White women may not be necessary for Negro women as far as what's practical to each individual. Smart and dumb is up to the individual. If you want what I call an attractive Negro woman, you might try a Negro woman that's a educator of math, or a medical doctor or chemist. And one that doesn't resort to sophism instead of objective, rational thought. Actually, you might want to use the word practical instead of dumb and smart. Dumb means ignorant, but all people aren't engineer degreed. Are all non engineers incapable of being practical to get sustenance for themselves to be labeled ignorant in general?

I've always heard that blond White girls were always hotter sexually than other types of White girls, and were always hotter for Negro men than other species of White girls. As a Negro race, I have had natural blond White girls act with passion towards me, but usually all I get is brunette White girls. I've had sex with a natural blond White race before, but the natural blond wasn't any hotter than the brunette White females I've had sex with, or the Latino and Negro girls I've had sex with.

I've heard Negro and White people say that once you race mix, you won't go back to your own kind. I can tell you as an all races race mixer, I will ball any race, heterosexual sex only, and hopefully the woman is a college/university graduate and works for a living, if I can pull such. There are many nice people in the world, and I don't see how people can only be into one particular race. Sex with all races is what I preach, and I brag about it. I've heard that Negro women who sex with White men don't want anything else. But my mulatto girlfriend of over 10 years ago has had sex with White men, as well as sex with Negro and Latino Indian men.

I've heard a statement from patrons of the gay community in S.F. that I believe is a generalized, collectivist concept. The statement is that once you're gay, you're always gay. Now, I know of men that were gay for way over 24 years, and since 1997 they haven't been gay to my knowledge. They only go for girls these years, and I never hear of them being gay, not ever. David Bowie, the rock star, has been said to be gay, but he has been married to a female for over 16 years, and a child came out of that marriage. So it seems all men who have been gay before are not always going to live totally gay. If any men who have been gay, then straight, go back to being gay, well, that doesn't mean all of the ex gays who are now straight will go back to being gay. There's just no way of telling.

I heard that transgender types who were originally men at first don't lay with females, but they do. One of my girlfriends used to sex with transgender types that were originally males. She even asked me to get a sex change so we could be a lesbian couple. I decided not to get a sex change, so I still have my original equipment, for all you girls that are biologically girls.

In Africa, some men have been told by the witch doctor of their community that to get rid of HIV disease, they will need to sex with 15 year old females so the disease will disappear from the infected male. When an HIV positive man goes to do such, he infects the 15 year old child with the disease, and doesn't get any cure whatsoever. Now there's one more disease carrier on the Earth. That type of collective dependence on witch doctors that possibly have no medical professional experience or rational thought process could be the death of the human race if not stopped.

I was told a while back by some ex friends that brown skinned Greek White girls don't sex and marriage with Negroes. When I was in the military, there were girls from the state of Rhode Island that were military members who were brown skinned Greek White girls, and they showed me their family photos. Every other picture in their family photos was of a Negro male who was said to be a brother in law, or one of their White girlfriend's husbands, and one of them said they had a Negro fiancé. I learned from those girls that many brown skinned Greek White race females from Rhode Island do go out of their way to marry Negro men. It's been said to be a tradition in Rhode Island among brown skin Greek families for many years. Personally, I'd be glad to get a pretty brown Greek White race female for a wife. But I believe these brown Greek White women in Rhode Island only go for the most dark skinned Negro male they can get. Thus, I don't make it with them, being high yellow skinned.

All gay people don't race mix. I've seen plenty of gay people who say they don't like anything for sex except for their own kind. The ones that were saying that were always White race gays.

I've heard all women that shoot heroin will only sex with a man if the man shoots heroin. I had a girlfriend that would shoot heroin everyday. And she didn't make me shoot heroin before any of our sex acts, or at all. The only women saying to me that they couldn't sex with a man if he didn't shoot heroin were woman that were racist against Negroes for prostitution sex, and/or a drug using 9th grade dropout.

Just because you heard a girl likes to be anal sodomized doesn't mean she will want sodomy. All girls that told me they like anal sodomy didn't let me anal sodomize them. Men, wipe off your prick when you pull out of the anal sodomy act. Girls, keep a feces free vagina so you can keep a husband longer.

Even with all the collectivism in the world, I managed to be an individualist seeker. I can truly, honestly say that I would love to see all the societal mores and taboos that my society has erected scrutinized until people would only speak the truth, and raise their children to do such. I have figured out how to approach living the life of an individualist without any pain or regret. A lot of times my society has already chosen who will be seen and treated as a winner or a loser. Many people actually want there to be losers in material possessions or status among humanity, so they can put themselves on a pedestal and walk around claiming they are preponderance over others because of what race, flag, or bible they believe in and worship. I don't claim to be a Christian, but that is what may get a person saved from wrath by God, not race or nation hatred, or misanthropy. For those like myself, who I don't believe are saved in God(Jesus), there is no excuse not to be Samaritan, or egalitarian. Help people out in their time of trouble if you can. Maybe you will get a neighbor to help you out too. Prove no one is going to treat you kindly. What's wrong with a new friend? A new friend isn't a problem with me, as long as that new friend isn't degenerate to bourgeoisie, and moreover, not degenerate to the concept of the leader if I or a potential new friend can't attain the position of an evolutionary, for instilling ambition in people to always want better than mediocre. I want evolution not only in technology, but in human relations as well. How many more will have to be victim of concepts like fear, jealousy, and tragedy, like the irrational can't be beat? How many people can't see truth for being hurt over someone's put down? I believe you may want to take some of the things I write here in these pages and examine them as to how you don't have to be victim of others in the society you live. There is no excuse for being hurt over anything another human says or does to you after the reading of this book project. I don't feel condescending when I say that if you're still humiliated by anything after reading this book, you'd almost have to be sub propagated or mentally disabled. If you're not mentally disabled and are still victimized by others in your society after reading this text, then read the whole text again. Read this text until you die, if that's what it takes for what I call pure rational thought to become a part of your agenda. Since when is purely empirical, rational thought made a fool out of? When is pure empirical thought for the rational made a victim out of, or victimized until it needs a victim? Treat my text as if your happiness, or your loved ones happiness, is really important, more important than looking at yourself as failure all your life. And more important than letting someone else's ways get you all ticked off. Perhaps with this text you can learn constructive criticism techniques, so as to entice your enemies to consider rational thought process, instead of perpetuating animosity that is only degenerate to fluid social harmony. I have tried to show how to come about feelings of pride in humanity, instead of humiliated, vindictive lifestyles, or the life of an unquestioning sycophant that may be disturbed by those that made light of icons/idols to the point the sycophant is viewed as irrational among the rest of their society. I have no heroes except for myself. Don't you wonder how that feels? I tell you, it feels great. I hope you will read this book until you are your own hero. Don't let the cynic deceive you out of your happiness. Or make you complacent enough not to see others feel great all their life. I believe with more happy people on Earth, the more peace we will have. I have peace of mind 24 hours a day. Take what I say and use it, so you can start to believe in it. It works for me.

Next, I will start to wrap up this text with my final thoughts on some more ways I'd like to motivate all the world to feel good about their life, and help to inspire good feelings in man . . . for mental utopia.

Epilogue

I've been mostly objective in my delivery of Mental Utopia so far. Now, I'm going to give my unexpurgated opinion in this next segment of my text. I will try to remain empirical in my commentary for you from here on out.

First, you are not a conservative or a liberal. You are either practical or impractical to get the pleasure you say you seek. I believe in order to assess life in an objective way without being influenced by irrational emotions, you will need to be empirical. Empiricism is to experiment and observe before coming to conclusions as to the nature of a subject or an object, and not to base your conclusions about a subject or an object on supposition or theoretic. The proper attitude for initiating empiricism is to think not to enter into conventionalist behavior without questioning that behavior. Why question convention? Because the innovators and leaders of this Earth questioned rigid tradition, there's been vast scientific advances in the Earth. Do you suffer fear and anger? Did you ever stop to question why you have fear and anger? If you take a nihilist approach to life, where nothing is as important as yourself, then how will you have fear and anger over things of this Earth? All people don't play by the rules for texts of psychology to be an accurate assessment of the human mind.

Who will you trust to make jobs for America? Will you trust people that control machines that maintain society to make jobs, or sophist politicians who have little if any education in science to make jobs? Why are you giving paychecks to those politicians who have no job certification in anything that the U.S. government needs for technical evolution of a human species? And what's wrong with abortion in the mind of republicans when they don't care if there's overpopulation of the Earth to the point of starvation of millions in Africa? Letting people procreate when there's only so much room on the Earth for housing and food production is asking for many people to starve to death, like politicians don't care. Indifference to overpopulation is asking for people to starve. Willing indifference to starvation is the same thing as murder, which is the same as abortion.

If republicans are pro life, then why does our U.S. government tolerate the tobacco industry? If republicans are pro life, why don't they push for legislation to reduce sodium content in food in the U.S.? Speaking of anti empirical waste of money, why does Rolling Stone magazine glorify rock/movie stars who really are not known to possess any engineering or medical/technical skills for upkeep of government, then criticize the republican party of America for glorifying millionaires and billionaires(of whom it is not known by me what value they have to the Earth)as Rolling Stone magazine does in some of their publications?

When someone makes you look anti empirical, you should embrace the empirical with happiness, not cynicism, and be glad that your flaw in rational thought was exposed for your sake, as well as for posterity. Empiricism shows evolution over flawed environment, and that someone cares enough to see evolution of human species is egalitarian, which is hardly anything to be cynical about. It shouldn't matter what race took steps for society to evolve, as long as ignorance of rational thought is exposed for all people to profit. Don't be anti empirical enough to look irrational as those who call their empirical superior a cynic because of looking like de-evolutionary relics of inertia to human species evolved over sophism.

With empiricism giving egoism temperance, and the concept of being vigilante, there may be no need for emotionalism outside of happiness, or emotionalism that may slave people into pain. At that point, how will there be anything such as Hell, intellectually or physically, or an instance where people consider themselves or others 'losers'?

If any college/university has Ayn Rand texts as electives or pre requisites, may the dean of that school consider this: you might have ego of a god, but do you have empiricism in problem solving technique, and can chemists defeat electromagnetism in the here and now? Empiricism seems to be the only way so far that people may yet try to conquer mortality(chemistry). And you can't miss or suffer what you can't measure.

If a text by Albert Camus called 'The Fall' is part of the school curriculum of a school that also teaches empirical science, then the continued use of such a text at that institution is contradictory to empirical, rational thought, since that text tells it's readers not to judge people, which is the opposite of empiricism, and also not instilling in students powers of critical thinking for problem solving. If God knows you have the judgment power to determine what is appropriate behavior for your benefit, then 'The Fall' is a sophist waste of student tuition, as is every major text that is nothing more than fictitious literature. Also, a text like Jean-Paul Sartre's 'Being and Nothingness' was big at one of the schools I went to. Can you really say anything about a text on being and nothingness except for I am, what it is is what it is, and we are able to sense what we sense, and that objects will be what they are until different, for such a text as 'Being and Nothingness' to get credit as a tool of educational process by some what people might have thought of as an egalitarian college/university dean, who looks to have no purpose more than ornamental instead of empirical?

With empiricism and nihilism, I don't need things to have to beat people out of material objects they value. Empiricism makes a justice so that when I see I'm not a slave to the temporal, then I get pride. You really can't own anything, and with empiricism, that which you want control of are things that it is practical to control for the instant, though unsubstantial and ornamental. I seek human race evolution through empiricism over the ornamental, for pride/self-esteem to be icon. Having pride from empirical, rational thought inspires the seeking of the primordial, for evolutionary process over pointless violence, and evolution over the condescending, for harmony. Harmony that shows you love yourself, and that can easily give and earn love. Egalitarianism seeks temperance to have more empiricism, the empiricism to be more objective, so that no pain(tragedy) is experienced when you find all people aren't guaranteed egalitarian, for self love realized.

Have you ever heard anyone say if you can't label them, you can't control them? Well, most human vigilantes are controlled by food. So that tells you to be a vigilante for yourself so you can control as much food as possible. Then you are more in control of your fate as possible. While politicians are plotting your fate, did it ever occur to you that you can control your fate as better as some politician? Why let them control the majority of your life? You see they usually don't go without what they want, don't you? Try being empiricist politics.

Predicting people's behavior is supposition. And, how is it wrong to impose empiricism on others when your government imposes their will on you? Weird is a supposition because all things we experience are of the Periodic table of the elements. Everything on the Periodic table of the elements is something that chemists say can't be created or destroyed, so it's been there since God made it trillions of years ago. Just because you're uncomfortable in a 'new' situation that doesn't make weird exist, because the elements that constitute that situation were always there, whenever the time you had your uncomfortable experience. So, are you going to continue to be offended by things that God made, things that were always the way they are, things that are now not proven to be weird? If weird doesn't obviously exist, then what is abnormal psychology? Nothing but gibberish. If all peoples idea of practical isn't the same, then how can the idea progress be the same in all peoples mind? Which gives you an excuse to be an individual, and stop castrating yourself out of what's comfortable just to live up to someone else's standards. Be an individual for your idea of progress, not stifled by race, flag, or religious icons that don't describe the true nature of Jesus. Perhaps live to be vigilante, or nihilist for your wants, not the wants of God or other people.

I've got some questions for the American Medical Association. If dopamine excess is said to be the cause of hearing voices, then how is it that methamphetamine users are not usually documented as hearing voices until they're hooked on methamphetamine, which is said by chemists to deplete dopamine? Why aren't those who said they hear voices tested with magnetic resonance imaging to determine if there is brain damage present in such a patient? Are psychiatrists afraid they will lose credibility, or some supposed prestige from their society, or paychecks to pharmacology nurses/ chemists?

How do doctors prove that fear is hereditary? Just like I've said before, I do believe that happiness is natural because all a human can instantly know of God's world is comfort of mere existence. That may suggest happiness is is hereditary. If happiness is automatically in your genes and chromosomes, then where does fear come from? Fear looks to be something you learn after birth, just like I said earlier in this text. You can't be born with fear and happiness at the same time. Otherwise, you'd reject your parents out of fear, and refuse to eat, or have a fit when your parents try to hold you. And you'd never get used to them long enough for you to learn to obey them, like you were a wild animal. All your emotions are learned, except for happiness that you were born with. I have shown you a few ways to beat emotion out of ruining your peace and social prowess with other people.

And, if you've got self-esteem, and supposedly born with that happiness, then how will you hurt or need to feel loved? Maybe you were tricked out of pride by sophisms of thinking you need to feel what other humans feel by anger from others that said you didn't give sympathy to people. What people say is love is a lot of times only lust.

About anger . . . a scientific research document I read said two groups of test subjects were both given a shot of epinephrine, and one of the test groups were given questions designed to provoke anger. The other test group was told jokes. The test group that was given questions to provoke them into anger got angry, and the test group that was told jokes stayed happy. The test group that got angry obviously had to learn to be angry, and their anger wasn't from the epinephrine. If lack of epinephrine is the basis for depression, how come the test group that got angry got angry while full of epinephrine? I believe you can't prove all of the same race or sex will act the same way under the same circumstances. So, there's no proof that any or all of any test group that gets the questions designed to provoke anger will guaranteed become angry, with or without epinephrine. But, I don't get angry at people like I used to, no matter what. Not only is that from empiricism and nihilism, but also from believing that leaders must be rational. You must want to become a leader, even if you get no prestige. It's your life, not somebody else's. Why only trust others for seeing things go your way, for your best interests?

Another question for medical doctors, particularly psychiatrists . . . how do you prove mania is illness when lack of emotion is said to be a major symptom of schizophrenia? Try to see the positive side of things. Accept responsibility for your behavior, or lack of. Don't let sophism from those who are said to be authority figures keep you buying into supposition, superstition, and living life naïve.

When you U.S. citizens buy illegal narcotics and marijuana, you are usually giving money to the enemy of the United States. The Taliban said they will beat Americans by making them slaves to drug addictions if America can't be beat by conventional warfare. Drug dealing is exactly how American government says North Korea has 5 nuclear warheads right now. And North Korea wanted to see America beat for many years, and says people of the U.S. are nothing but dogs. Some Koreans, including some that live right here in America, say that all Negro and White people aren't human, and are nothing but monkeys(said by a Korean I met who was actually serving in our American military while I was enlisted). For all you that deal illegal drugs, and all who use illegal drugs, you may not be able to stop nuclear warheads as good as you beat the police. These Persians and Pakistanis and Central/South Americans that are dealing illegal drugs to America, they don't want you in their country, they don't won't to birth your children, and they will kill you if you trespass in their territory, especially you Negroes that are so hot for drugs that three Negroes a week are going to the penitentiary all across America, and the Persians, Pakis, and Latinos from outside America are only laughing at it. It's time for America to wake up or be beat. It's time for pride, instead of running to the liquor store and the pot dealer every time you don't feel challenging to the world at large. Did you ever notice how people that are running the country are mostly sober, while those said to be in poverty are the majority of what's in the drug program? If life is hard for you, you might as well try work until you're $3000.00 a week, instead of lying that poverty in the housing authority on SSI/welfare is hardship. Most SSI and welfare recipients had just as much time in the day for college courses as everybody else, and you know not to have children before proper education.

Speaking of educating yourself, I was told by what I consider a plebian that I possess a doctor's education. Why do I consider that statement plebian? Because if a doctor's education is guaranteed intellectual preponderance, then all the chemical and mechanical engineers in the world that are doctors in engineering would have the same rational capacity as each other to the point they'd all have their name on a blueprint of something primordial in engineering, instead of the majority of them dying in obscurity. And if this what I call plebian were talking about medical doctors, well, all medical doctors aren't guaranteed able to do the same medical breakthroughs as those noteworthy enough to distinguish themselves from obscurity, and be considered evolutionary. Is it guaranteed in the capacity of any medical doctor to be of empirical, rational thought, enough to guarantee that any and all of them can conquer emotionalism outside of happiness, or drug dependences if they are under the influence of such? I've seen doctors that smoke tobacco. Do doctors that smoke tobacco seem empirical and rational to you? What's a doctor's education got to do with repetitive study habits for the intellectual grasp of empiricism? Any doctors that seem empirical in thought and behavior, were they always doctors for you to be stopped from empiricism for yourself? I never even received an associate degree, so I'm no doctor.

I also heard what I call a dunce, and this dunce was telling me that they didn't think I had a White race's intelligence, because I didn't kiss uncle tom. I must say, all White races didn't tell me to give them preferential treatment, as many never even needed me to care about them. Furthermore, if a White race's intelligence is guaranteed preponderance to any and all Negroes and Orientals, then why are there Whites with no chemistry education among White races, and why are there Negroes and Orientals with employment, if all the White race was interested in getting and giving preferential treatment to only White races? Also, when was all White race product guaranteed empirically correct for any and all Negroes and Orientals to use, and for Negroes and Orientals to guaranteed be able to grasp empirical method of thought from patronizing of such product, for Negroes and Orientals to give prestige to any White just because they were White? Do uncles believe Negroes and Orientals should be kissing White ass to anything White when it's obvious that all the White race's names aren't on all blueprints that make Western civilization? Do uncles prove White races have more ambition to provide upkeep of Western civilization than Negroes and Orientals, and that Negroes will guaranteed get and keep employment if they lick uncle? I believe many uncles are uncle from being under the influence of a White race's pretty white skin before the uncle could think pride, something I really feel has been brainwashed into millions of Negroes (perm hair straightening). Why would you uncles bow to mere White humans who have no guaranteed power of redemption? I think Jehovah is White, but what guarantee do you have that Jehovah gives special treatment to White races, or that him being White is how he got to be of his powers? Considering the word vigilante, prove that it would be wrong to be more intelligent and more physically powerful than all humans, Satan, Jehovah, and Jesus, for the concept of licking uncle tom to be seen as anything more than irrational compared to the concepts founded by the men and women of all races who contributed blueprints for the devices that make today's Western civilization. And all doctors, whether they be engineers, chemists, or medical doctors, are not all races race mixers, which isn't empirical, or rational minded. So much for doctor minded and White minded statements supposedly describing intellectual preponderance. If all White race are of the constituents of a White man's education, uncle Negroes, then why isn't all the White race's idea of empiricism for the practical of the same idea? And even if empiricism is a White race's invention, prove that all White races are capable of empirical method of reasoning, or all White race are capable of chemist degrees. Are all chemists empirical at all times? Well, all chemists are not guaranteed race mixers. And anti race mixing is irrational. Dogs and cats can race mix with different race humans, and animals aren't more rational than 3 year old humans. Anti race mixing is irrational. Pride is rational if it comes from empiricism. Are all chemists of White race blood? No. Then, some Negro chemists are empirical enough for their lab managers. You say a Negro chemist isn't supposed to be seen as empirical enough, compared to non chemist degree White races, to the point you give prestige to anything White race more than anything Negro race? That's irrational as Negroes that can't have pride unless a White race gives them a complement, or a sex act. But then, what is pride about the irrationality of racism? So much for laughable, sophist uncle toms who hate their own race. So much for worshipping race instead of empirical method of reasoning. Most all Negro race in America that understands and lives English composition, English literature, and White race heritage, has some sort of White race intelligence. And, how can you lie and say all White race has equal prowess in problem solving? Empiricism is the real supremacy in thought. Race doesn't guarantee empiricism.

If you stress empirical competence, then drug test elementary, high school, and college/university teachers, as well as pharmacists, chemists, medical doctors, and dentists for illegal and/or mind altering drugs. I don't want to be poisoned.

Keep abortions legal. A woman has the right to do what she wants with her body, and it's not anybody else's right.

No to corn ethanol for fuel. Corn ethanol gives more carbon emissions than gasoline. I suggest you tell your representative in congress to investigate this.

For Christians and egalitarians alike, employers should give lie detector tests to potential employees to see who's racist, so these bigots can be documented for the world to see on internet, and for unbiased leaders among us to be identified and given the prominence they deserve in life.

There is no higher social status than the rational mind that doesn't depend on the opinion of others for self-esteem. I feel good every day because I am rational to the point I don't need to be counseled as to what was my value to society and myself. When seeking empiricism, I give value to myself and I make decisions that I am happy with, and usually see all my decisions turn out well. My intention for humanity is to see empirical method of thought and behavior proliferate in all the world, which fosters rational minded societies. Concerning people that I don't share many common values with, I can live among them in peace, because I want to see peace, because I'm not living the life of a victim anymore thanks to empiricism. That is true justice. For myself, and the world, and future generations.

I hope you enjoyed this text. Give it to your friends, and your enemies as well. If you will, request that this text be made part of the educational system in not only the United States of America, but all over the world.

What I have written here I feel are the constituents of a pleasant stay on Earth, for anyone that wants to be a leader of themselves, and perhaps others. Those that aspire to make leaders, or that call themselves a teacher designated to the cause of uplifting minds out of degenerate emotions that blind people to peace and love should investigate what I say here. Those that truly want to see people concerned with positive mental outlook, and want to rise above the commonplace animosities that people have been prone to rigidly perpetuate, should choose to instill what I say in all humans. Those that care for mankind should not let those that adhere to the parochial, whatever social conduct that is, keep you from objective, rational thought. When greeting people, try to deal them the truth, as you would want from others. Show the world an egalitarian, hopefully so they won't become slaves to the sophisms of misanthropy. Some have been fooled into thinking that life is going to be some sort of burden. I want to defeat sophism in general, as it may blind aspirations in youth, and in all those that want to see a triumph over inertia in thought and action. Defeat the inertia of degenerate societies that suppress evolution of a human species out of freedom from mental pain with the poison of sophist irrationalism. Peace on Earth . . . for love . . . for mental utopia.